Facing the Depths

Exploring Psyche through the Art of Masks

Tina Azaria

Psychology / Jungian / Women Authors

ISBN:098922581X
ISBN-13: 978-0-9892258-1-6

Cover Art: *Door to the Depths* © 2017 Tina Azaria
Cover design by Tina Azaria

DEDICATION

I dedicate this book to fellow explorers of the inner depths and to those who follow the inner spark, wherever it may lead.

CONTENTS

Acknowledgments   i
Introduction   ii

1	A Masking Journey	1
2	Mythic Art	11
3	Evolution of Masking	24
4	Art of Transformation	37
5	Exploring Psyche	53
6	Gathering Tools	60
7	Embarking on the Journey	69
8	Layers and Levels	80
9	Meeting the Guide	86
10	A Mask is Born	96
11	Illuminating Symbols	104
12	Decoding Messages	117
13	Out of Darkness	123
14	Enter the Void	140
15	Initiatory Descent	132
16	Reclaiming the Rejected	151
17	Awakening Instincts	158
18	Conscious Approach	171
19	Opposites Unite	179
20	Shadow Integration	188
21	Exploring the Boundaries	196

TINA AZARIA

LIST OF FIGURES

Figure	Title	Page
1.	Childhood Clown Drawings	iii
2.	Jester Drawing	vi
3.	Juggler Drawing	vii
4.	Halloween Clown Mask	4
5.	First Performance Mask	6
6.	Medusa Mask	7
7.	Inner Alchemy Drawing	90
8.	Face Cast	97
9.	Face Form	98
10.	Light Mask	100
11.	Void Mask	126
12.	Void 1	128
13.	Void 2	128
14.	Star 1	128
15.	Star 2	128
16.	Horned One Mask	160
17.	Prayer Stick Front	216
18.	Prayer Stick Back	216
19.	Venus of Willendorf Drawing	217
20.	Ancestor Stones	218
21.	Initiation Hall Murals Scene 1 – 4	219
22.	Initiation Hall Murals Scene 5 – 10	220

ACKNOWLEDGMENTS

I extend my deepest gratitude to all of my teachers from the Sonoma State Depth Psychology Master's program for their wise guidance and continual encouragement to explore psyche and share my discoveries. I especially thank Dr. Laurel McCabe for introducing me to the mysteries of embodied mask work and Dr. Mary Gomes for stewarding the research and experiments that form the basis of this book. I also want to thank all of my students for having the courage to show up and let me take you with me on wild adventures into uncharted creative territory. I am thankful for the explorers who have tread this path before me and the mask spirits themselves, who are the true authors of this work. Finally, I thank my family and friends for believing in me and my work.

INTRODUCTION

Imagine for a moment… A dark night with thousands of stars illuminating an indigo sky. A large central fire before you, the faces of your community glowing in concentric rings surrounding the blaze, circling out toward the darkness beyond. A slow, steady drum beat lulling you into hypnotic states of reverie. When suddenly, a cast of masked figures enters the fire circle. You watch, enraptured as beings from another world enter your reality and transport you to an enchanted realm beyond this realm, to a time outside of time. Life morphs before your eyes into a dreamlike, eternal landscape where the dramas of the ages play out.

Your mind clears as your attention is focused singularly on the figures and scenes before you. Your imagination expands, carrying your soul aloft on wings of delight. Your heart opens wide as emotions flood through you. You feel cleansed of daily concerns and present to a deeper, more ancient side of humanity. Connected by invisible threads to all life, you feel at one with the universe. You experience a moment of transcendence in the presence of the Masks. Ephemeral yet profoundly transformational. As the performance ends you feel renewed, deeply satisfied, and somehow, more whole from the experience. This is the power of the Mask.

In the following pages I invite you to journey with me as I explore the mysteries of personal transformation, catalyzed by creating and donning masks within sacred rituals. We'll dig into the roots and history of masks and see how they've been used throughout time periods and cultures. We'll get to know the change-inducing Trickster archetype and examine theories on psyche's transformation, as it relates to the art of masking. Then, I give you a peek into my masking laboratory where I share bits and pieces of my records and describe the results and conclusions I've reached through conducting creative, investigative studies with masks.

This book is derived from my psychology master's thesis entitled *Masks and the Art of Transformation: A depth-psychological study* (2012) and the years of teaching that have followed. The work I describe is a work in progress. I do not claim to be an expert or to have all the answers. If you're looking for certainty and flawlessness, you're not going to find it here. What you will find is work that stretches the boundaries and takes leaps into the deep end of the inquiry pool. I encourage you to hold this work with curiosity, kindness and the respect that the art of masking requests of all who wish to dip their toes into this pond.

But First…A Personal Creation Story

While my formal mask-oriented research began in 2009, as a graduate student in Depth Psychology at Sonoma State University, my relationship to the mask, and its partner, the Trickster, have been life-long. My earliest memories of childhood are permeated with the presence of the Trickster archetype and images of the mask. As a young child I slept under a bed quilt covered with images of mask-faced clowns who filled my dreams and waking consciousness. I spent a considerable amount of time drawing clowns and creating carnival-esque stories. Trickster, a shape-shifter who embodies duality, signifies transition, and is often depicted as a clown-like figure, is a natural companion of the mask, as I explain in further detail in Chapter Four.

Figure 1. Childhood Clown Drawings

I came to mask work as a natural progression of my study of depth psychology and my creative processes as a visual artist and performance poet. (I have often said that I did not choose this work, but it had chosen me long before I ever realized it). I was fortunate to be raised in a large extended family with a rich oral storytelling tradition on my mother's side. (Which, not so coincidentally, helped offset the misfortune of having suffered complex childhood trauma – trauma I've largely healed through expressive arts therapies). Both my Irish/Swiss-Italian grandfather and my Slovenian grandmother were immersed in oral storytelling traditions rooted in what they referred to as the "Old World."

As a result of these traditions, I grew up with an awareness of and connection to the mythic realm, a special place where ordinary and non-ordinary reality meet at an invisible boundary. This liminal place, this realm between realms, has long intrigued my intellect and sparked my imagination. I believe this liminal state, this borderland between the known and unknown, the conscious and the unconscious, is the place many artists, poets, dreamers, visionaries, and healers go to for inspiration and guidance. This is the place we journey to when we don a mask.

As I entered my teen years I remained in steady relationship with the clown, altered into the images of jester, joker, and harlequin. I continued creating art inspired by this fascination and I embodied (unknowingly) some of the Trickster's boundary-crossing, shape shifting qualities. As a punk rock influenced youth in the 1980s, I was constantly changing my physical appearance in dramatic ways: cutting, shaving, and dying my hair many colors of the rainbow; playing with dramatic make-up and creative costume-clothes. My outward appearance was always changing. And still is.

From Personal to Transpersonal

I began writing Trickster-inspired poems and making Trickster-ish art in which I gave myself complete creative license to express anything, particularly topics pushed away into the personal and cultural unconscious – into the shadow. I let the stirrings of my psyche come out in words and images that were unfiltered and, at times, subversive and confrontational. It was me, it was my voice and vision, yet it was more than me. Somehow I knew, even then, that there was something taking place that was beyond my personal frustration and teenaged angst. I had intense experiences of a transpersonal nature, but did not have a framework or vocabulary to understand them at that time. My work with masks has deepened my understanding of transpersonal phenomena. I believe masks create a doorway into our deepest selves and beyond, into transpersonal realms, igniting experiences which can catalyze dramatic changes in personality.

At age sixteen I went to New Orleans, to the jazz festival. There were myriad Mardi Gras masks decorating and animating the city with an other-worldly personality. I was inexplicably drawn to and mesmerized by New Orleans, the "City of the Saints," and the fantastical masks it proudly displayed everywhere. I purchased several ceramic copies of Venetian masks as well as a pair of brass comedy and tragedy masks which became my most prized possessions. Back home in Denver, Colorado I hung the masks on my walls and began actively collecting masks, jesters, joker cards, and harlequins. I even got a jester tattoo coinciding with my transition into living for several years as a traveler.

Figure 2. Jester Drawing

I continued to draw and paint masked figures and jesters well into my adult life and created my first wearable plaster mask in my late twenties, as an undergraduate art student. The work you're about to encounter began formally in 2009 and has continued and expanded to this day. I hope you find intrigue and inspiration in the work that follows. It has catalyzed incredible transformations for myself and my students and I invite you to consider how the mask might find its way into your life and work a bit of its magic on you.

Figure 3. Juggler Drawing

1 A MASKING JOURNEY

The angels and demons, the fairies and fiends, are inside each of us
It is we who bring them out into the world
We breathe our life into them and give them form
It is we who create the hells and heavens, the pain and the ecstasy here on Earth
The battle between light and dark, between good and evil, is within us all
The internal drama plays itself out on the world stage
And we harm and heal, hate and love, accordingly
~ Tina Azaria, personal journal entry, May, 2009.

Starting at the Beginning

This book arises from a spark of inspiration so enchanting, it sent me on a deep expedition into the vast terrain of the human psyche. It completely captivated my attention, compelling me forward into an ever-deepening relationship with the mystery and power of the mask. I have found that masks enhance our expressive powers, enrich culture, and give life to imagination. Working with masks can bring insight, emotional release and healing - ultimately leading to expanded self-awareness and a deeper sense of wholeness.

The studies and, what I can best describe as "encounters," that follow stem from my personal research and experiences, informed by many great thinkers and explorers of human consciousness and the arts, as well as by my students. The imaginal practices and methods I describe herein are changing who I am in unexpected ways– from the vast reaches of my internal landscape to my external relationship with the outer world. I am passionate about this powerful work and hope to inspire others to engage in the transformative art of sacred masking practices.

Masking our Way into Psyche's Depths

This is a voyage into the modern intersection of masks and sacred rituals, known simply as "masking" or masquerade. The rituals I share with you are a meeting of ancient expressive and healing art forms that can bring genuine renewal to individuals and to culture. It's certainly been transformational for me and my students and I'm excited to show you what I've discovered in terms of working with masks to facilitate lasting changes in the human psyche.

Working with mask and myth in a ritual setting has the ability to bridge the conscious and unconscious minds and reveal deep interior experiences that lie below the threshold of everyday awareness. Bringing unconscious material into consciousness can be a profound therapeutic experience, if the appropriate healing container is present. Working with the unconscious is no joke, so I implore you to take this work seriously and create the appropriate container, as described in Chapter Seven.

Shadow Work

The combined use of mask, myth, and ritual is particularly suited to the discovery, investigation, and ultimately, incorporation of the *shadow* – the unknown, disowned, and dissociated aspects of psyche – weaving them into a dynamic and integrated whole. I have found that, with the appropriate intention and approach, mask work holds the power to help *anyone* bring forward and assimilate fragments of personality hidden deep within.

The work described in this book is grounded in depth psychology and art therapy theories and methods. We'll touch upon these topics briefly, for context, though an in-depth look at either topic is well beyond the scope of this book. While a background in depth psychology and expressive arts therapies is helpful in understanding this material, it is not necessary. I will lay out the foundational knowledge areas for you in the coming chapters and the bibliography will point you to further reading. Depth psychology generally refers to the work founded by Carl Jung and extended by countless others who have furthered the work he began. You'll get an overview of this powerful form of psychology in the coming chapters. The mask work itself is an example of depth psychology in action.

Crossing Boundaries

At its core, the work herein is about exploring the boundaries between inner and outer, self and other, the known and the unknown. The language of the unconscious is symbolic. That's why working with archetypes and symbols can be indispensable when it comes to healing psychological and emotional wounds and gaining deeper self-understanding. Often, symbols and archetypes can remain too abstract to really benefit the personality on a practical level. This is where masks come in as particularly helpful. Masking, as an *embodied* expressive arts medium, is an especially good way to learn about archetypes and symbols as they apply to *you*. By sharing my own personal experiences, I hope to demonstrate the merits of working with masks to better understand the impersonal, universal structure of archetypes and symbols that are available to guide each of us on our journey to wholeness.

The Art of Transformation

Since I can remember, I have been captivated by the art of disguise, the role of the clown, Trickster, and shape-shifter in society, which I later discovered are all catalysts of transformation and facilitators of psychic border-crossing. Through my investigations, I have come to see that my life-long personal fascination with masks (see introduction) has to do with the more-than-human quality that infuses them. The experience of self and other generated by masking is particularly transformative. A special relationship is created between mask and wearer, which I explore in-depth in this book.

Although I have had a life-long intuitive connection with masks and shape shifting characters, it wasn't until 2009, when I became a Depth Psychology graduate student that I began to peel back the layers of why the symbol of the mask has always been so important to my psyche. *The Mask is the consummate symbol of our ability to change and transform.* My personal path has largely been about transition and transformation, so I began to see that masks were an apt symbol. But masks are more than a symbol of transformation; they're an instrument used *for* transformation.

My primary curiosity about masks has to do with the archetypal, or universal change-producing undercurrents that permeate mask work, a concept I will be expanding on throughout this book. The mysterious power of the mask has enthralled me since childhood and has become the foundation for a lifetime's worth of work.

Early Encounters with 'Self and Other'

I still remember the Halloween I was three years old. I decided to be a clown that year. I instructed my mother in painting on my clown face mask to mimic the clowns covering my bed. To this day I remember my surprise and delight at seeing my masked face reflected in the mirror. I remember feeling giddy, silly, wanting to giggle, act goofy, and let my inner clown out to play. It is the first time I recall experiencing the sensation of being me and not me at the same time. In that moment with the mask I am me and I am other. As I look in the mirror, I see me and more than me reflected back.

Figure 4. Halloween Clown Mask

What is this me/not-me, self and other experience induced by the mask? This is the compelling question that brought me to my investigative work with masks. Some of the persistent curiosities that drive my work include: What happens when one intentionally dons a mask to consciously shift identity? Who is the mysterious "other" that arrives when we put on a mask? And how does the experience of this mysterious other relate to the trance-like state induced by wearing a mask? I hope to begin addressing these questions and more throughout this book - though admittedly, the more answers I seek, the more questions I come away with!

In the first semester of graduate school, I was introduced to masking within the container of a sacred ritual by Dr. Laurel McCabe. We spent three class periods: first making plaster masks, then decorating them, and finally each student was asked to participate in a masking ritual. Following is an excerpt from my journal entry, written immediately after the masked ritual to give you a sense of the work:

> I step into the ritual container and invite the spirit of the mask to enter.
> I don the mask and wait in stillness until I feel a shift in the quality of my attention and in my body. Then I surrender to the waves of energy pulsing through me, rocking my body back and forth in a steady rhythm. Words flood my mind which I am hesitant to speak at first, but I can't seem to stop them from pouring out. I say things about opposites, balance, rhythms. I am only partially aware of what I am saying.
>
> Then, as suddenly as it came, the energy is gone. I feel alone in my body once again and know my performance is complete. I take the mask off and sit down feeling bewildered and energized by the experience. I am in a heightened state of awareness. My body tingles and I am in an excited state. (Azaria, personal journal entry, November, 2009).

Figure 5. First Performance Mask

This experience was so captivating, I soon made another mask and then another. I ended up creating a masked performance using music and spoken word to recast the myth of Medusa as contemporary tale of betrayal and empowerment, weaving in the mythic roots of the tale which are believed to lie with a real-life queen from Libya, North Africa. In the creation and the performance of the myth I experienced the presence of both myself and the archetype, as if our voices were weaving together to create a story that was cathartic, renewing, and somehow integrative for my psyche.

Afterwards members of the audience reported a sense of entering a deep state of relaxation, total immersion in the story, and even altered states of consciousness from *witnessing* the masked performance. I, the performer, emerged from the experience feeling centered, energized and somehow more whole. A mysterious transformation occurred and I was compelled to delve deeper into the mystery of masking.

Figure 6. Medusa Mask

From there I went on to teach undergraduate psychology students and then further, to teach mask work in my community to people of all ages and backgrounds who are interested in personal transformation. I have seen the potential of masks at work and in action, bringing healing to myself and members of my community.

During my foray into mask work, my primary objective became exploring the impact of masks and masked rituals on the psyche. All of the in-depth mask work described in this book came out of the following curiosities around the psychological, emotional, spiritual, and physical effects of masks on the wearer. I have been specifically interested in examining:

1) Experiences with masks and masked ritual performance that are transformative and/or healing;

2) The psychic events associated with the creation of the mask and the mask performance;

3) The effects of the mask's imagery on psyche; and

4) The types of understanding such encounters with masks bring.

This book is an exploration of these questions. Throughout the following chapters I attempt to answer the above questions through my experiments with masks.

Why Masking Matters

I believe that self-exploration will increasingly become the most critical work of this century and many different avenues and tools are needed to help us each accomplish this important work of self-discovery. I believe that the revival of the ancient practice of masking offers a unique avenue for personal development by facilitating psychological, emotional, and spiritual insight. This work has the power to help us assimilate important personal and collective stories of wounding and triumph and reconnect us with the essence of what it means to be human.

Our world is changing quickly. Rapid advances in technology, accelerated hybridization of cultures, and global environmental crises are forcing us into uncharted territory in both our individual and collective realities. I believe that significant change must begin with the individual, for it is a corpus of individuals which comprise a society. Societies collectively comprise a global population, a population currently in need of deep and permanent shifts towards balance and renewal. How do we address the disorders within and without in a way that contributes to personal and collective healing and repair? I believe we humans have done this important psychic restoration for millennia through sacred expressions such as masking rites and rituals.

I entered into masking with the intention of integrating the divergent and contradictory aspects within my own psyche which create internal conflict and confusion. I have found mask work to facilitate a direct link into my own unconscious where valuable pieces of psyche have been hiding and lying fallow. Through my work with masks I have been integrating these fragments into a meaningful mosaic, capturing and conveying my past experience and future vision. I have found no better way to do this than by working with masks, myths and rituals, as people have done since the dawn of human culture. The embodied nature of mask work takes my psychic stirrings from the abstract level and grounds them into physical reality and into my physical body in a way no other art form has yet been able to do.

I believe masking is a vestige of the past that continues to hold social and cultural relevance, even in today's fast-paced, techno-centric world. In this book, we'll take a deep dive into mask work as a powerful contemporary form of art therapy that has ancient and fascinating roots. What I have found has left me with further questions, beckoning me deeper and opening new horizons of inquiry. It is my hope and intention to revitalize the practice of what I view as *Shamanic Art Therapies*, with masking residing at the core of this transformational work.

Myth, mask, and sacred ritual unite to provide a time-honored method for promoting initiatory experiences, as I explain throughout this book. The contemporary value of sacred mask work is that it can be tailored to accommodate any life circumstance and cultural orientation. I believe that these are just a few of the many reasons why ritual mask work has continued to be practiced from ancient times into the present day, in cultures around the globe.

It is only through penetrating into our own shadows that we can begin healing our individual wounds. When we heal our personal wounds, we begin healing the collective wounds that threaten the well-being of humanity and planet Earth. I believe the work of healing can be not only inspiring and creative, but can also involve the elements of playfulness and fun. For me, mask work is a profoundly important and transformative form of play with a fascinating history and intriguing future potential. I believe it is inherent and accessible to everyone and that it comes from and connects to a place deep within our psyches. I believe that masking itself is archetypal.

2 MYTHIC ART

In order to understand my particular approach to working with masks, it's helpful to have some background information on the structure of the human psyche from the perspective of depth psychology. This is the most basic of primers. For further reading, see the list of references at the end of the book.

Setting the Stage

Psyche

The *psyche* can be described as the central hub of cognition, emotions, behavior, and even the intelligence of the physical body. According to pioneering psychologist, Dr. Carl Jung, the psyche has three layers: the *conscious mind*, the *personal unconscious*, and the *collective unconscious*. The conscious mind consists of everything that resides within our conscious awareness. The personal unconscious is an accumulation of personal material that lies outside of immediate awareness. It holds content that has either been repressed or has simply never registered in the conscious mind. The collective unconscious is an innate part of the psyche shared by all humans across times and cultures. It is a vast world, undifferentiated and unstructured in comparison with conscious reality. It can never be completely assimilated into consciousness. The collective unconscious is the deepest layer of the unconscious mind, is transpersonal in nature, and is composed of archetypes[1], which will be explained further in this chapter.

Psyche and Symbol

The unconscious mind communicates with the conscious mind through symbols and images. Because the inherent language of psyche is symbolic, it can be challenging to decode and understand the messages that arise from the unconscious.[2] The unconscious can only be observed indirectly, through the by-products of its inner workings which are released into the conscious mind by way of symbolic expressions such as dreams, reverie, and right-brain dominant activities such as art which allow for symbolic communication to emerge.[3]

With metaphor and symbol we are able to apprehend and appreciate aspects of human reality that lie beyond our ability to fully understand, intellectualize, or control.[4] Creative expression at its best is a *spontaneous symbolic manifestation of unconscious impulses and instincts* which operate outside the bounds and limits of the cognitive, rational mind.[5] Noteworthy thinkers, such as C.G. Jung and D.H. Lawrence, expressed strong sentiments that excessive rationalization has alienated humans from the natural world and from our own souls, leaving us with afflicted and disconnected individuals and societies.[6] Using art and imaginal exercises as a means of restoring balance to ailing individuals and communities is an ancient practice rooted in shamanic traditions.[7]

Our imaginal faculty connects us to the infinite realm of the collective unconscious, which includes yet transcends our rational and emotional functions.[8] The capacity of the human imagination to form symbols is what makes conceptions of soul, spirit, or divinity in any form, possible.[9]

Jungian analyst James Hollis[10] addresses the vital role of the human imagination: "Without the archetypal imagination, we would have neither culture nor spirituality…" According to Jung[11], the numinous nature of the human psyche is revealed through symbolic forms and gestures that bubble up from the deep unconscious realms. Psychologists have called this aspect of psychic functioning the *archetypal* or *mythic imagination.* James Hollis addresses this important psychological faculty and its relationship to human culture and notions of powers greater than the human mind:

> It is the archetypal imagination which, through the agencies of symbol and metaphor and in its constituent power of imaging, not only creates the world and renders it meaningful but may also be a paradigm for the work of divinity.[12]

Jung[13] insisted that there exists in all humans a religious instinct, an intrinsic drive to connect with a higher power, with something or someone that transcends human limitations. He supported this theory with the fact that every single civilization on the planet, past and present, has some form of religion – a set of spiritual beliefs and sacred rituals. Due to the universality of religion, Jung viewed it as a manifestation of the collective unconscious which allows humans to relate to the awesome and incomprehensible powers of the numinous through symbols, metaphor, and imagination.

The archetypal or mythic imagination is the means by which an individual perceives and creates patterns and brings a sense of order to the chaotic experience of the undifferentiated unconscious. It is also the means by which the individual participates in those vast and mysterious energies of the cosmos of which we humans are intrinsically a part.[14] It is our mythic imagination that not only facilitates our conception of divinity, but connects us to our ancestors and the myriad cultures that populate our rich and diverse human world. Stephen Larsen[15] describes the importance and contemporary relevance of participating in mythic thinking:

> Yet even now mythology emerges as the legacy of a whole planet. To understand other people and other cultures and the images we share – and fail to share – with our fellows, we must relearn an aboriginal language, the universal tongue of the human imagination. With its inexhaustible vocabulary of symbol and story, it is at once our ancestral birthright and the ever-brimming well of dreams into which we look to find our future.

The Mythic Realm

Throughout history, human cultures across the globe have been in relationship with the unconscious via connection with the mythic realm, sometimes referred to as the dream time, the archetypal realm, or the other world.[16] By engaging this non-ordinary reality through art, myth, sacred ritual, and other practices our ancestors had access to information and wisdom that helped guide, protect, heal, and inspire their communities. Although it is ever-present, contact with this realm has withered in modern times. Contemporary culture has generally discouraged our awareness and appreciation of the world of imagination.

We may have lost immediate access to this faculty, yet I believe it is always with us. Entry into the mythic realm, the realm of imagination, is still available to all who seek it. There are many doors and pathways that lead to this vast and mysterious world. For me, nature, stories, myths, rituals, and the expressive arts have provided the most direct link with the mythic world populated with the archetypes and symbols that have shaped human kind for millennia. The work described in this book represents my personal process of bringing these modes of mythic access together in my own self-awareness practices. This passage from *The Mythic Imagination*[17] eloquently captures the essence of this other realm:

> As in the long-ago campfire or longhouse ceremonies of our ancestors, when the dream breaks into this world from that unknown one, it brings with it another kind of illumination: the light of the mythic imagination. Seeing into the other world, using our imagination, requires a different kind of seeing – with the inner eye, the mind's eye-that we have almost, it seems, forgotten how to do. And that is why, as the legends tell us, that the other world is the "bright world." Its images, the myth forms, are lit from within, "self-luminous." Simply to contemplate them kindles the imagination, and they are contagious, they may illuminate other human minds.

There *is* a realm of consciousness beyond our waking reality. There are doorways between the worlds of waking and dreaming, of rational and imaginal thinking, for each world needs something from the other. Entry into the other world, the mythic world, requires the imagination that is very much alive in us as children and often dies away as we move towards adulthood. Children engage in storytelling and mythmaking easily and effortlessly. As adults, it is something we frequently must relearn.[18] I was fortunate to maintain a life-long connection to the mythic realm, which I believe is not simply a vestige of childhood. My personal experience has shown me how vital and necessary imaginal processes are to sustaining a deeply meaningful and balanced life.

Masks have been used since ancient times to transport both wearer and audience to a realm beyond every-day reality. It is for this very reason that masks have long been associated with sacred rituals and ceremonies such as rites of passage, as I describe in further detail in Chapter Four. Throughout this book I describe personal excursions into the mythic realm which prove to be initiatory experiences facilitated by work with masks, myths, and sacred rituals. It is important to note that these are not culturally defined practices passed down to me through a community of elders.

The masked rituals I describe emerged directly from my own depths and are deeply personal. However, I believe the personal is, in practice, intrinsically tied to the collective, as the collective is fundamentally made up of the individuals who comprise it. The personal and collective, as well as the inner and outer, are engaged in an ongoing dynamic relationship which causes each to inform and influence the other on a consistent basis.[19]

The Inner Archetypal Theater

Within the depths of our psyches we each have a collection of archetypal energies, an inner pantheon, that shape and inform our lives. Inside every individual there lives an inner cast of characters who together compose our unique, multiplicitous personalities.[20] These dynamic aspects of personality move in and out of awareness, unconsciously affecting our thoughts, moods, and behaviors until we consciously locate and name them.[21] I believe the mask acts as a unique vehicle for embodying these archetypal energies and giving them tangible shape and form. Once substantiated, the archetypes within can be purposefully accessed and explored, as I will attempt to demonstrate throughout this book.

Archetypes

Jung described *archetypes* as universal patterns, or fundamental building blocks, of the psyche.[22] The archetype can be thought of as a blueprint that informs and structures individual and collective human experience and behavior. Through years of empirical research and clinical observation, Jung came to believe that the archetypes are autonomous constituents of the collective unconscious, the part of the unconscious mind shared by all people across times and cultures[23]. By definition an archetype is a *ubiquitous prototypical psychic inheritance.* Just as we inherit physical characteristics based on a "blueprint" of the human body, we inherit psychic characteristics based on a "blueprint" of the human psyche. In Jung's words:

> [T]here exists a second psychic system of a collective, universal, and impersonal nature which is identical in all individuals. This collective unconscious does not develop individually, but is inherited. It consists of pre-existent forms – the archetypes.[24]

Archetypes manifest cross-culturally as images, symbols, and motifs found repeatedly in myth, religion, and art throughout recorded history. There are numerous examples of archetypes such as The Great Mother, The Wise Old Man, The Divine Child, The Warrior, The Wounded Healer, and The Trickster, to name a few. Archetypal motifs include The Hero's Quest, The Night Sea Journey, The Battle of the Opposites, and so forth. Experiences such as Love, War, Death, and Creation are also archetypal. The study of archetypal patterns provides a helpful framework for understanding and describing the intricacy of contemporary psychological experiences. Myths and other archetypal stories, such as fairytales, present a mirror reflection of prototypical human trials and triumphs which can guide and comfort us in times of transition and uncertainty. While archetypes are universal experiences, they are complex and multifaceted patterns which, paradoxically, manifest uniquely in each individual.[25] In other words, the Trickster is known to wear many faces and costumes that have been personalized by different cultures and individuals. Yet at its core, the patterns and dynamics attributed to Trickster are constant and universally recognizable. Author Robin Robertson[26] provides an apt description of this phenomenon:

> [A]rchetypes are activated in many, perhaps all, human situations. As we personally experience the world through the archetypes, the archetypes are given a particular, highly personal form.

I believe that rituals, myths, and masks together serve as a secure container for archetypal energies, allowing us to uncover and work with these potent more-than-human forces without the danger of identifying ourselves with them – a phenomenon known as archetypal possession. We can put the mask on, work with the archetypal energy, and then take the mask off, returning to our known self with fresh insight and expanded awareness. We can dip down into the inner realms of the personal and collective unconscious and, ideally, bring back the treasures therein.

Assembling the Cast

Ego, Persona, and Conscious Identity

As described in depth psychology, the *ego* is comprised of all that is held within conscious awareness. It is the seat of individual identity, the personal sense of "I" as understood by the conscious mind.[27] The *persona* is likened to a mask, the face(s) shown to the world, which helps an individual function in society.[28] The word persona derives from the Latin word for masks worn by ancient actors to indicate the particular role they played.[29] The persona functions as a mediator between the individual and society and is not a disguise, but rather, an identifier.[30] In simple terms, it could be said that the ego is who we believe ourselves to be and that the persona is how we choose to present ourselves to the world.

Masks have been said to conceal conscious identity (ego and persona) in order to reveal something much deeper.[31] At its most basic the mask is a symbol of our ability to disguise and transform our persona. The complete shift in identity that is possible through donning a mask makes it particularly suited for moving beyond the confines of the known self, the ego and its various personae, to enter into the archetypal realm. The mask is an apt medium for exploring boundaries and investigating the role of appearance in the experience of change, particularly changes in identity.[32]

Masks push our awareness beyond identification with the ego and persona by concealing the everyday self by means of disguise. The mask is the most widespread form of disguise used throughout the world.[33] With masks we can change our most basic identifying factor, our physical appearance. The human face is the primary means of recognizing and identifying one another. This physical change can be intense and even disturbing. Think of a very young child seeing the familiar face of their mother suddenly hidden by a mask. Her familiar appearance is visibly altered into something completely different and unfamiliar. Now, imagine the intensity of upset that could be induced by such a change in appearance. If you've looked at yourself in a mirror with a mask on, or seen a familiar face covered by a mask, you probably know what I'm talking about. This is an example of what I mean when I say the physical change in appearance can be disturbing.

The Self, Individuation, and Alchemy

The word alchemy is as familiar as it is mysterious. It conjures visions of ancient scientists attempting to change an inferior substance (lead) into a superior one (gold). Yet the art of alchemy has always addressed more than just the outer transfiguration of metals. Ancient alchemists were equally concerned with the inner transformation of the human psyche.[34] In the early twentieth century, C.G. Jung began correlating alchemical methods and symbols with a psychological process he termed *individuation*.[35] Individuation is the development of wholeness over a lifetime and leads to the emergence of the *Self*.[36] Jung described the Self as the totality of the psyche which unites the opposites and holds everything together in balance and unity. The Self is the center of the psyche, yet it transcends the boundaries and limits of the psyche.[37] Alchemical symbolism provides a useful framework for understanding the process of psychological transformation and advancement toward wholeness. I will be using the language of alchemy to help describe the transformative process I experienced by engaging in ritual mask work and I will define and describe alchemical terms throughout this book.

Casting the Shadow

The *shadow* represents all that is unknown and undeveloped in a person or a culture. It can be psychic content that is repressed or simply undiscovered by the conscious mind.[38] The shadow contains features of a personality that go against the grain of the customs and moral conventions of the social environment. It is the unconscious side of the ego and is connected to shame. We all have a shadow side, it is not only unavoidable, it naturally occurs as part of normal psychological development. The shadow is an adaptive mechanism that allows us to function in a world rife with moral conflict. It allows us to act out parts of our nature that are unsavory to an ego needing to conform to moral standards that may go against our deeper instincts.[39]

Renowned Jungian analyst Marie-Louise von Franz[40] explains that The Shadow is simply a mythological name for all that resides within which we do not directly know or see. The split between the known and the unknown creates an inner and outer duality that often causes us to divide the world and everything in it into polarities - light vs. dark, good vs. evil, and so forth. The shadow, representing the dark, unlived, and repressed side of each of us is the converse of ego consciousness. It has been said that we carry a mask in front of us (persona), we cast a shadow behind us, and that the ego stands in between.[41]

The shadow consists of many aspects and layers. There is a personal shadow, a cultural shadow, and a collective shadow within us all.[42] The personal shadow contains parts of us that would ordinarily belong to the ego if they were integrated, but instead have been split off from the ego and suppressed because they are contrary or not in synch with our ideas and feelings about ourselves and the world.[43] The cultural shadow is made up of the repressed and unknown psychic content of a group of people: a family, a community, a race, a country, etc.[44] The collective shadow is comprised of repressed and unknown material that resides in the collective unconscious. The collective shadow holds the summation of all the fear and pain inducing aspects of existence for the entire human race since the beginning of time as well as all that is unknown on a collective level. It is considered to be the primeval aspect of the shadow. It is less differentiated than the other layers of the shadow.

There are some personal, cultural, and collective stories that are so painful we struggle to hold them in our awareness. So we bury them deeply in the shadow where they await our conscious excavation. To reach a state of balanced wholeness, we must, at the very least, bring the buried personal shadow material out into the light of consciousness. Doing this helps to diffuse the shadow's power to unconsciously move and motivate us in undesirable ways. I believe that the ritual use of masks holds a unique ability to bring personal and cultural shadow material into the conscious mind so it can be worked with and integrated into our awareness.

Mask – Concealer and Revealer

The power of mask work in addressing shadow material, in part, lies in the anonymity it provides. In their seminal work on masks from around the world, John Nunley and Cara McCarty[45] point out the shadowy behavior that can accompany masking traditions: "The power of anonymity gives us the protection to behave in ways we otherwise might not, to act aggressively or break the rules." In the language of depth psychology, masks help bring forward aspects of personality that the ego may find threatening or distasteful, aspects normally relegated to the shadow lands of the unconscious. They go on: "Masks empower us to divulge our hidden, true selves or secret thoughts, exposing inhibitions or personality traits that we ordinarily contain or feel unable to express."

Masking helps us move beyond the confines of ego identity and perhaps even facilitates the conception of new identities for individuals and societies. The implications of this level of transformation, the redefining of self and society through masquerades, is very exciting. The idea of using masks to reframe one's concept of themselves is not new. In fact, scholars believe this to be at the heart of ancient and indigenous masking traditions.[46] The ability of masks to bring a renewed sense of identity is part of their efficacy and is embedded in masking traditions, as recounted in the following quote[47]:

By taking the sounds and sights of a natural world animated by the world of the spirit and reproducing it in a controlled environment [masquerades], human beings (and men in particular) felt empowered. Such empowerment provided the necessary confidence to invent culture and to assign meaning in a world that was, and is, always verging on chaos, danger, and death. The mask provided security in an unpredictable world. It allowed for human emotion to be displayed and negotiated in times of joy and stress. Its strength has been renewal itself.

End Notes

1. Robertson, 1987; Stein, 1998; Weinrib, 1991
2. Johnson, 1986; Raff, 2000; Swartz-Salant, 1995
3. Johnson, 1986; McNiff, 2004; Robertson, 1987
4. Hollis, 2002
5. McNiff, 1992
6. Jung & Sabini, 2002; Lawrence, 1921
7. McNiff, 1992
8. Hollis, 2002
9. Hollis, 2002
10. Hollis, 2002 p. 6
11. Jung, 1938
12. Hollis, 2002 p. 7
13. Jung, 1938
14. Hollis, 2002
15. Larsen, 1990, p. xviii
16. Larsen, 1990
17. Larsen, 1990, p. xix
18. Larsen, 1990
19. Larsen, 1990
20. Stein, 1998
21. Larsen, 1990
22. Stein, 1998
23. Jung, 1967; Stein, 1998
24. Jung, 1953, p. 43
25. Stein, 1998; Weinrib, 1991
26. Robertson, 1982, p. 105
27. Weinrib, 1991
28. Larsen, 1990; Weinrib, 1991
29. Stein, 1998
30. Nunley & McCarty, 1999
31. Napier, 1986
32. Napier, 1986
33. Napier, 1986
34. Swartz-Salant, 1995
35. Swartz-Salant, 1995; Raff, 2000
36. Stein, 1989
37. Stein, 1989
38. Stein, 1998; Weinrib, 1991
39. Stein, 1998
40. von Franz, 1974
41. Stein, 1998
42. Shalit, 2008; Stein, 1998; von Franz, 1974
43. Stein, 1998
44. Jung, 1959; Neumann, 1969; Sidoli, 2001; Stein, 1998
45. Nunley & McCarty, 1999, p.16

46. Elston, 2004; Napier, 1986; Nunley & McCarty, 1999
47. Nunley & McCarty, 1999, p. 38

3 EVOLUTION OF MASKING

Working with mask and myth in a ritual setting has the unique ability to bridge the conscious and unconscious minds and reveal deep interior experiences that lie below the threshold of everyday awareness. Bringing unconscious material into consciousness can be a profound therapeutic experience if the appropriate healing container is present. Myth, mask, and ritual together provide a time-honored method for promoting initiatory experiences. Further, ritual mask work can be tailored to accommodate any life circumstance and cultural orientation. I believe that these are just a few of the many reasons why ritual mask work has continued to be practiced from ancient times into the present day. In this chapter, we're going to survey sacred and secular mask use throughout cultures and time periods and explore the link between mythology and the art of masking. The following topics are important for understanding the masking processes described in later chapters.

Enter the Mask

Masks symbolize our ability to change and transform. They have the ability to pry loose our grasp on mundane reality, pushing us over the boundaries of the ordinary and into the realm of imagination and possibility. Masks have been worn in healing ceremonies, sacred rites, carnivals, and theaters since time immemorial. Using masks to shift identity is an ancient and ubiquitous practice.

Archeological findings indicate that masks have been around for more than 30,000 years.[1] Cave paintings and sculptures from France contain the earliest known depictions of masked beings engaged in masquerade activities.[2] Masks appear on every continent and in every era. The universal use of the mask throughout cultures and time periods indicates it as an object of considerable cultural significance. That it has survived, intact, into the present day signifies a profound connection between the human psyche and the art of masking.

Masks and Sacred Ritual

Early evidence of mask use suggests that it has deep roots in sacred ritual.[3] In Paleolithic times, hunters performed masked rituals before and after the hunt to obtain blessings and assistance from the spirits and ancestors.[4] Masks have served as an integral part of shamanic healing rituals and an essential tool in the healer's medicine bag.[5]

Masked ceremonies have long been performed during transitional times associated with significant changes in the lives of individuals and societies.[6] Rites of passage such as birth, marriage, and death, as well as rituals of renewal associated with annual cycles and seasonal changes mark occasions for masked rituals and celebrations often referred to as masquerades.[7] Masquerades provide an important avenue for communal celebration, artistic expression, and the reenactment and preservation of cultural myths. Most cultures throughout history have set aside considerable time and significant resources for masquerade activities.[8]

Masks as Medicine

Masking appears as a key component in healing rituals and curing ceremonies performed across the globe, from the Americas to Africa, the North Pole to New Zealand.[9] Powerful healing forces are channeled through masked healers and dancers with the intention of restoring balance to the ailing individual and the entire community – which is impacted when even one of its members is ill.

To honor the North American land I occupy, I will share two brief examples of native North American practices. These examples come from Northern New York, where my husband is from and the Rocky Mountain region, where I am from.

The False Face masks used by the Haudenosaunee, or Iroquois tribe of Western New York and Ontario, Canada are primary to the tribe's healing ceremonies. Carved wooden masks are inspired by dreams or visions of spirits. When a mask appears, the future healer is obligated to create it, and is then inducted into a quasi-secret society of healers. Each healer has a distinct mask, inspired by their dream or vision, which is worn during sacred rituals performed to restore health and balance to ailing individuals.[10] The tribal healing ceremonies are always performed with the False Face masks.

Masks are a central component in the Diné (Navajo) Nightway Ceremony. Also known as the Night Chant, or Klédze hatál to native speakers, this sacred ritual is one of their most important and involved healing ceremonies.[11] It is performed to treat prolonged illness, particularly mental illness, psychological and emotional maladies, and anything affecting the head.[12] The ceremony involves the use of sacred myths, prayers and chants, hundreds of songs, numerous dances, and a special collection of shamanic masks.[13]

Traditionally, the masks are made from buckskin obtained from a deer. There is much ritual and taboo around the construction of the medicine masks. Each one is designed to represent the specific Diné gods and goddesses that are associated with the Night Chant. According to the instructions handed down through generations, a full set of twenty masks must be made in just one day. The masks are created to be permanent tools in a medicine man's collection and he will often use the same ones throughout his career. A couple of the masks are impermanent and created for a single healing ceremony. These will be destroyed once the nine-day ceremony is complete. The masks are worn by the Diné dancers to invoke the Holy People during certain ritual components of the ceremony.[14]

Masks and Initiation

Anthropologist Victor Turner[15] observed, during his extensive cross-cultural studies, that performance activities, such as masked rituals, do not occur at random. They appear at times of crisis and renewal. Sacred masked performances tend to constellate around *liminal* occasions - when continuity and stability are threatened by change and life is suspended in a precarious balance between old and new. Masked ceremonies arise to facilitate and ease times of personal and collective transitions.

Times of transition can be dangerous, threatening the stability of individuals and societies. The powerful forces of the cosmos and the spirits of the earth and of ancestors are invoked through masked rituals where they are entertained and appeased so that the next phase in the cycle can be safely and successfully navigated.[16] Rites of passage such as birth, marriage, and death, as well as rituals of renewal associated with annual cycles and seasonal changes mark occasions for masked rituals and celebrations often referred to as masquerades.[17] More information about initiation and its rites can be found in Chapter Four.

The mask has long been used as a conduit for communion between the individual and something larger, be it the spirits, the gods, or the greater human community.[18] I believe the connection between masking and sacred ritual has remained intact from antiquity into the present day due to the mysteriously powerful connection between self and other that occurs in the presence of the mask.

Masks in Ritual Theater

A distinction has been made between masquerade masks used in rituals of renewal and rites of passage and theatrical masks used to entertain. I would argue that even within the bounds of pure entertainment, masks help us transcend the limitations of daily life and connect us with deeper longings and images of who we are and who we aspire to be. Those who research masking traditions often present conflicting views that result from the tendency to see mask wearers as either true incarnators or mere dramatists, without seriously considering that both of these functions may occur simultaneously.[19] Kerenyi[20] insists: "[T]he function of the Greek actor or poet was not to represent some imaginary being but to evoke one that actually exists."

Despite the proposed differences between ritual masks and theater masks, anthropologists worldwide acknowledge commonalities in sacred and secular masked performances.[21]

Characters, symbols, and archetypal motifs show up cross-culturally despite ethnic, religious, and political differences present in societies with vital masking traditions.[22] For example, the struggle between good and evil; death and rebirth; the incarnation of spirit; and the antics of the Trickster archetype are common motifs found in masked rituals and theater from cultures spanning Africa, the Americas, Asia, India, and Europe.[23] In Asian performance traditions the boundary between sacred ritual and secular theater is far more permeable than in Western traditions, where more discrete lines have been drawn.[24] While masking practices in Asia are as rich and varied as the cultures they stem from (Bali, China, Korea, India, Indonesia, Japan, Nepal, Sri Lanka) an underlying acceptance of using masks to explore alternative states consciousness and connect with divinity is present throughout.[25]

The mask in Western theater has its roots in ancient Greece and Rome. Originally associated with the Greek god Dionysus (known as Bacchus in Rome), the mask was used to disguise a mere mortal and transform the person into a higher, divine being during ecstatic Dionysian festivals.[26] While theories abound about the transformation of mask use from celebratory worship to dramatic personification, the true nature of this shift is yet unknown. In time, the mask was relegated to a tool in the actor's repertoire. It became a second face wherein a second identity is allowed manifest on the stage.[27] In the theater, ancient and modern alike, the mythic world intersects with everyday reality, opening the way for numinous experiences to occur for both performer and audience.

While it is common for sacred masked rituals to assume an air of respect and even reverence, secular mask use (such as Commedia Dell'Arte, Mardi Gras, Carnival, Halloween, etc.) is often done as a parody of ritual traditions, turning the established order upside-down for a time. As a contemporary acting teacher who trains his students with masks, Ken Elston[28] makes a strong case that certain ritual components are inherent to mask work regardless of the intention or context. He contends that, regardless of whether the masked performance is secular or sacred, reverent or profane, it is always infused with transformative potential and a depth of meaning. He explains that the mask acts as a conduit, helping wearers or actors enter into the creative state. He describes the link as follows:

The bridge between the two [sacred and secular] manifests in the way ritual connection to the mask exposes us to our humanity and something larger than ourselves, in this case the audience. But it is possible that communion, in so far as it defines the creative state, suggests a fusing that makes the *creative state-self* bigger than the *pre-creative state-self.*

Elston[29] describes the creative state as being characterized by body-mind unification, complete presence in the moment, heightened intuition, sensitivity to impulses, and transcendence from everyday concerns. He speaks of the "ritual inhabitation of the mask." For Elston and many others in his field a mask is not simply worn, it is inhabited.

Keith Johnstone[30] is another performance instructor who teaches mask work to actors. He makes it entirely clear that his intentions are not to casually slip on a mask and simply pretend to be another person. He maintains that masks are capable of inducing trance states and that the "...genuine Mask actor is inhabited by a spirit" He describes numerous experiences of the masks used in his classes mysteriously appearing to transmit information to the wearer. He gives several examples of this. "I remember a Mask I'd just made. A student tried it out and turned into a hunched, twisted, gurgling creature. Then, a latecomer arrived, picked up the same Mask, and the identical creature appeared."[31]

Based on decades of investigation he has found that each mask used in his workshop displays a specific personality with unique accompanying desires. He explains that with the right approach the mask will "switch on" and the character will manifest its presence, informing the wearer of its nature and preferences as it guides behaviors and effects emotions. He and his students have noted a marked change in consciousness and an awareness of the presence of another personality while wearing a mask.

He has found that masks have what he refers to as a "mind of their own," making it particularly challenging to cast them in plays. They are consistently unpredictable and do not adhere to scripts. It is important to note that he and his students report the masking experience to be both therapeutic and transformative. Johnstone[32] emphasizes the importance of creating and maintaining a safe environment while working with masks. This is analogous to the idea of containment in depth psychology and one of the primary reasons I do mask work within the clearly delineated boundaries of a ritual setting, as I describe in greater detail later chapters.

Masks and Myth

The use of masks in conjunction with myths is so wide-spread that some scholars believe the two are inseparable. For example, mask making has long been inspired by characters and events found in myths. Likewise, the retelling of myths is frequently accompanied by masked performances that portray the most important cultural narratives.[33]

In his book *The Way of the Masks*[34], Anthropologist Claude Levi-Strauss examines what he considers to be the inseparable link between masks and myths in the North West Pacific Coast native culture. He says that their masks "cannot be interpreted in and by themselves as separate objects, but, as with myths, must be returned to their transformation set: the set of masks and their associated myths in which each echoes and transforms the others."[35] He goes on: "Each type of mask is linked to myths whose objective is to explain its legendary or supernatural origin and to lay the foundation for its role in ritual, in the economy, and in the society."[36] From the Americas, to Bali, to Greece masks have systematically accompanied the sacred mythologies enacted in rituals and theater.[37]

Myth and Psychology

Myths, like masks, are inherently symbolic. It is with our mythic imagination, defined in Chapter Two, that we must view mythology in order to render it useful for self-awareness and psychological growth. While there is a tremendous amount of material written on mythology in general and the use of mythology in psychology particularly, I have selected only a few examples in order to maintain brevity and focus.

Both Freud and Jung took giant leaps to begin understanding human nature in terms of myths.[38] Freud's seminal theory, which formed around the Oedipal tragedy, connected psychology early on with myth in a concrete and tangible way.[39] The original Greek word *mythos* is related to the English word for plot.[40] In his book *Healing Fiction,* psychologist and founder of Archetypal Psychology, James Hillman[41] elucidates the power of mythos:

> [A] mythos is more than a theory and more than a plot. It is the tale of the interaction of humans and the divine. To be in a mythos is to be inescapably linked with divine powers, and moreover, to be in mimesis with them.

Again we find a link between myths and masks in terms of their ability to help humans navigate a relationship with the divine. Haida artist Robert Davidson says of this: "When I create a new mask or dance or image, I am a medium to transmit those images from the spirit world...masks are images that shine through us from the spirit world."[42] The same thing has frequently been said about myths.

Historian and theorist Mircea Eliade[43] was a foundational thinker and prolific author on mythology and ritual who has been exceptionally influential to the fields of religion and depth psychology. Eliade observed that, in traditional societies, myths, such as those retold at masquerades, describe the essence of the primordial events upon which the natural and human worlds are established. In Rites of Renewal, masks were worn to reenact the myths of the creation of the cosmos. Eliade[44] maintained that all myths speak of origins and in that sense "[M]yth, then, is always an account of a *creation.*"

This concept has been extremely important to the field of depth psychology. Freud's *Oedipus Complex,* for example, was used to explain the origin of a certain childhood neurosis he believed mimicked the mythic tale of Oedipus killing his father and marrying his mother.[45] Freud's early work with myth was influential on Jung[46] who developed the link between psyche and myth well beyond his mentor's. Freud had a limited view of mythology, seeing it as related solely to pathology and wish fulfillment caused by repressed libido.[47] Jung, on the other hand, seeing mythology as contributing to normal psychological development, moved the role of myth to areas well beyond of the realm of pathology.[48]

Psychologist June Singer[49] explains that Carl Jung viewed mythology as the symbolic language of the collective unconscious. The relationship of myths to the collective unconscious is plain: the collective unconscious is comprised of archetypes and mythology, with its plots and characters, is founded on archetypes.[50] Masks function as a container for the symbols and archetypes of the unconscious and pair seamlessly with myths to convey the deeper mysteries of existence, such as the mysteries of creation, destruction, and transformation.

Part of the power of myths is that they provide an archetypal model for life experiences common to all people, ancient and modern and can create restorative conditions for individuals and groups. Myths can reveal an overlap of individual experience with the universal experiences of all humankind, and in so doing, provide comfort and a sense of direction and meaning within the difficult experiences of human suffering. Mythology not only serves to explain mysteries of the outer world, it also gives form and structure to the inner world of psyche.[51] Jung believed that the best way to learn about archetypes is to study myths.[52]

Mythologist Joseph Campbell[53] spent his career relating world mythology to the human experience. He explains that myths indeed serve to illuminate the human condition, but more importantly, they elicit emotions and actions in the audience by conveying dramatic, archetypal situations which everyone can relate to.[54] On an individual level, myths together with masks allow the archetypes to express themselves and to thereby come alive within us, so that we can experience them directly.

In my own experience, combining myths with mask work has been useful in helping me illuminate and integrate unconscious narratives that underlie certain beliefs. Together, masks and myths provide a map through unfamiliar territory, such as initiatory experiences, that may be new to me, but are actually as old as humanity itself. Myths help us make sense of confusing situations and can model character traits necessary to specific trials, such as mustering patience, courage, and forgiveness in the face of adversity. We can see our own life experiences in the stories of mythic characters, which helps us to feel less alone and isolated in our difficulties. Myths help us to universalize our experiences and make meaning of suffering while masks help us ground this understanding into a physical experience.

Myth and Ritual

Joseph Campbell[55] noted the similarities between mythology and ritual in his description of the standard progression of mythic narrative and its relationship to common ritual structures. The formula for both is based on the concept of rites of passage which includes separation, the liminal phase where the initiation proper occurs, and the return, which are explained in greater detail in the next chapter. Ritual provides a means for enacting a rite of passage, embodying a transition, and delineating a specific time as sacred.[56] Rituals are imbued with symbolic meaning and non-verbal expression of initiatory phenomena such as death and rebirth. The symbols encountered in a ritual, whether they come from within or without, can be used to broaden one's concept of oneself and the world, as well as inspire continual reinterpretation of self and life.[57]

Mythology and ritual are ancient side-by-side practices, found cross-culturally, that are frequently accompanied by the use of masks. Joseph Henderson[58] describes the importance of mythology and ritual for contemporary people. He explains that the patterns frequently found in many mythologies correlate with patterns that occur in the development of consciousness in an individual. He further points out how the mythological patterns mimic certain actions in rites and rituals. In this way myths often guide and inform ritual processes. Thomas Moore[59] describes the historical connection between myth and ritual. He illustrates this with the fact that, in many traditional societies, when the creation myths were told the act of creation was simultaneously celebrated and revered through ritual enactment of the myths, often with the use of masks. Moore[60] suggests that mythology speaks to important felt experiences in a non-literal way and that the accompanying ritual actions, such as ritual death and rebirth, serve to integrate the experience on deeper levels.

I hope you're beginning to see the depth and complexity of how ritual mask work can have a profound effect on the psyche. It not only opens doorways of self-understanding, it actually helps facilitate psychological transformation for individuals and entire cultures. We'll dig deeper into the mysteries of transformation in the next chapter.

End Notes

1. Nunley & McCarty, 1999
2. Nunley & McCarty, 1999
3. Elston, 2004
4. Nunley & McCarty, 1999
5. Matthews, 1902; Nunley & McCarty, 1999; Ritzenthaler, 1969
6. Turner, 1979
7. De Jong, 1999; Nunley & McCarty; 1999; Phillips, 1978
8. Ehrenreich, 2006
9. Nunley & McCarty, 1999; Matthews, 1902; Ritzenthaler, 1969
10. Ritzenthaler, 1969
11. Matthews, 1902
12. Faris, 1990; Matthews, 1902
13. Faris, 1990; Matthews, 1902
14. Matthews, 1902
15. Turner, 1979
16. Nunley & McCarty, 1999
17. De Jong, 1999; Nunley & McCarty, 1999; Phillips, 1978
18. Elston, 2004
19. Napier, 1986
20. Kerenyi, 1960, p. 154
21. Elston, 2004
22. Elston, 2004; Nunley & McCarty, 1999
23. Emigh, 1996; Nunley & McCarty, 1999
24. Emigh, 1996; Nunley & McCarty, 1999
25. Emigh, 1996; Nunley & McCarty, 1999
26. Kerenyi, 1976; Nunley & McCarty, 1999
27. Nunley & McCarty, 1999
28. Elston, 2004 p. 225
29. Elston, 2004, p. 228
30. Johnstone, 1979, p.143).
31. Johnstone, 1979, p. 165
32. Johnstone, 1979
33. Emigh, 1996; Larsen, 2000
34. Levi-Strauss, 1982
35. Levi-Strauss, 1982, p.12
36. Levi-Strauss, 1982, p. 14
37. Emigh, 1996
38. Hillman, 1983
39. Black & Mitchell, 1995; Hillman, 1983
40. Hillman, 1983
41. Hillman, 1983, p.11
42. Nunley & McCarty, 1999, p. 30
43. Eliade, 1963
44. Eliade, 1963, p. 6
45. Black & Mitchell, 1995

46. Jung, 1961
47. Black & Mitchell, 1995
48. Jung, 1961
49. Singer, 1972
50. Jung, 1964
51. Jung, 1964
52. Larsen, 1990
53. Campbell, 1964, 1968
54. Campbell, 1964
55. Campbell, 1964, 1968
56. Shorter, 1996
57. Shorter, 1996
58. Henderson, 1964
59. Moore, 1992
60. Moore, 1992

4 ART OF TRANSFORMATION

Transformation is a fascinating issue to consider, one that is both timely to our development as a global culture and an age-old concern. The actual mechanisms involved in psychological transformation are a bit of a mystery. Much research has been conducted on the mysterious inner workings of transformation and over the past century models have been developed to help us better understand this elusive yet crucial topic.

Betwixt and Between - Transitions and Liminality

Rites of Passage

Victor and Edith Turner[1] define *rites of passage* as "The transitional rituals accompanying changes of place, state, social position, and age in a culture." They divide the process into three phases: separation or detachment from an earlier fixed state; the marginal, or liminal, state of ambiguity that falls between; and finally, aggregation, or reincorporation into the collective in a visibly changed way.[2] Masked rituals help give form and structure to these universal, yet often obscure psychic and cultural processes by bringing them into conscious awareness – helping the initiate to recognize, celebrate, and ultimately, integrate these important times of change.

The French folklorist and ethnographer, Arnold van Gennep, was the first social scientist to study transitional phases which precede the emergence of unprecedented conditions from previously well-defined, fixed states.[3] Through his investigation of ancient rites of passage, Van Gennep opened a new line of inquiry into the phenomena of liminality and cultural transformation that has continued to develop. The concept of liminality as the "betwixt and between" is now applied more broadly to decisive cultural change in which previously prescribed ways of being give way to unexpected ideas and relationships.[4] Liminality is not only about transition states, but also the inherent potentiality that accompanies them.[5] Of this Victor and Edith Turner[6] say:

> In limina throughout actual history...we tend to find the prolific generation of new experimental models - utopias, new philosophical systems, scientific hypotheses, political programs, art forms, and the like – among which reality-testing will result in the cultural "natural selection" of those best suited to make intelligible, and give form to, the new contents of social relations.

Masks have long been used to help individuals and societies successfully traverse times of transition. Masks have been an integral part of initiation ceremonies and rites of passage. When I began working with masks I had no idea where this work would lead me. In time, the process began to reveal itself as an initiatory experience. It is important to note that I did not begin my masking experiments with the intention of igniting an initiatory experience. It evolved organically and was guided by the masks themselves and by the archetypal symbols they brought forward from my unconscious, as illustrated in later chapters.

Initiation

Initiation, from a psychological standpoint, addresses areas of arrested development, the places where adults have failed to mature.[7] All psychodynamic theories on the origins of arrested development are based on the underlying premise that the ego structure fails to achieve a stable identity through the normal course of development.[8] While early pioneers Freud and Adler emphasized external, environmental factors as the primary cause of arrested development,

Jung had an endo-psychic approach. Jung argued that how an individual reacts and internally relates to the external event is more important than the event itself.[9]

Jung described the ego as a complex characterized by a continuity of character that spans the lifetime of an individual. As a complex, it is subject to the same distortions of consciousness found in other complexes.[10] Jung believed that the developing ego is stunted not only by previous external events (traumata), but also by the subsequent ego-based fear of taking the next naturally occurring developmental step forward. The ego suffers from a normal, protective reaction known as psychic recoil. The pattern of recoil begins to dominate the personality and the ego-consciousness is unable to abate it without sustained and focused effort on all fronts. If the recoil becomes fixed into a habitual pattern, the outcome is arrested development in the areas of the personality impacted.[11]

The resultant state is described as a renegade tendency which isolates the individual from the typical, normative models of relating to others.[12] The process of maturity in certain areas of the personality is stunted. The archetype associated with this arrested behavioral pattern is that of the *puer/puella aeternus* the image of the eternal, self-renewing youth. Jungian analyst and author Joseph Henderson[13] describes the pattern well when he says "[The puer aeternus] embod[ies] a self-renewing youthfulness as an end in itself, never reaching, and by its very nature never intending to reach, maturity."

The Archetype of Initiation

In depth psychology initiation is described as an archetypal pattern which moves through psyche and propels us towards growth and transformation.[14] It is an impersonal, collective energy that rises up in the individual psyche in a way that is unique and reflective of personal circumstance and stage of psychological development.[15] Initiation is a universal, archetype-driven pattern that requires appropriate containment if one is to successfully transverse the process of transformation and, ultimately, arrive at a new phase of life. Because the narrative of psychic development unfolds over time in a non-linear, often irrational manner, it can be difficult to track its movement. That is why guides and maps are invaluable for illuminating the universal patterns that occur within the initiation process.[16] I believe the ritual enactment of myths and the invocation of the ancestors, gods, or archetypes through masks have long served as a guidepost in this murky realm.

In the modern world, many of us lack the structure and support surrounding initiation once available to our ancestors. Many of us do not have the collective community rituals that have marked the initiation process for thousands of years. My work with masks and myths in a ritual setting is intended to bridge this gap and provide a compass, rooted in the archetypes and symbols of the collective unconscious, for navigating the mysteries of the liminal realm.

Myths and rituals provide much needed guidance for the initiate and are thus an important part of any culture.[17] Patterns can be identified in initiation stories even though the individual experience of initiation will always be inimitable.[18] Initiation is a ritual act whereby the divine is directly experienced in the form of symbols that embody a multiplicity of fluid meanings.[19] Later in this book, I will illustrate how working with masks sent me on a psychological initiatory journey where I encountered the numinous nature within, and perhaps beyond, my own psyche.

Transformation

Symbols - Agents of Transformation

As explained in Chapter Two, the unconscious mind employs symbols to communicate with the conscious mind. Writer and Jungian analyst Anthony Stevens[20] describes a symbol as an image or object whose value lies in the emotions and meanings it invokes. In other words, the power of a symbol lies in the emotional charge and the depth of meaning that arise from it and *this* is what distinguishes a symbol from an image or object that does not serve a symbolic function. Stevens[21] explains that symbols are never invented by the conscious mind. They are always generated within the unconscious and are then released into consciousness via symbolic expression such as dreams, reverie, and the arts. Symbols come into conscious awareness spontaneously and exist beyond the devices of the ego.

The complexity of symbols lies in the fact that they refer to experiences and concepts that cannot fully or accurately be represented in physical reality, in the world of matter. Symbols point the way to mysteries, to things that lie beyond that which we can grasp with our mind, with our senses, with our reason, and logic. In his book, *Ariadne's Clue*, Anthony Stevens[22] quotes Jung to help further illuminate this thorny concept:

> [A symbol is] the best possible formulation of a relatively unknown thing, which cannot for that reason be more clearly or characteristically represented…[it is] something more and other than itself which eludes our present knowledge.

Here, Jung is basically saying that symbols refer to ineffable experiences and, therefore, can only partially convey the essence of that which they seek to describe. To further complicate matters, symbols do not arise in a neatly laid out order that can be easily tracked by the logical mind. This makes it difficult to study the complex anatomy of an individual psyche. Decoding the symbolic language of psyche does not easily lend itself to linear thinking. Working with symbols requires one to think differently. In *Symbols of Transformation* Jung[23] defines two types of thinking. The first style is directional thinking, which has a clear purpose driven by the will of the ego. It is linear in nature. The second kind of thinking, fantasy thinking, is driven by the unconscious. Here, the ego steps back and the unconscious engages in fantasies that follow an undirected and spontaneous path of associations.

In his book *The Mysterium Lecture's: A Journey through C.G. Jung's Mysterium Coniunctionis*, Edward Edinger[24] discusses a third way of thinking that he calls network or cluster thinking. It involves a union of both types of thinking, directed thinking and fantasy thinking, and joins them together to form a third approach. It has a purpose but it is not linear; instead, it focuses around a central image or idea. Thoughts move out in a radius and are always brought back to the central point; building up a network like a spider builds a web. This is the way to work with symbols in order to illuminate the unconscious. It is the net result of network thinking that eventually yields a rich and descriptive picture of the psyche and the process of individuation. It is the pattern of interconnected images that together create a detailed map of one's psyche.

Jung's psychological theories assume that a symbol alone can bring about all the essential changes we observe in personality and behavior.[25] For example, a symbol can arise during a time of personal crisis and through working with it, an individual can receive the comfort, guidance, and strength needed to overcome the crisis. Belief in the transformative power of symbols, although held with skepticism in many psychological circles, has a long and respectable history preceding Jung, going back to early Greek philosophers such as Plato.[26]

My work with masks pivots around the theory, demonstrated by Jung throughout his career, that symbolic work is transformative. Masks have the ability to crystalize a symbol, turning it into an image and object that can then be worked with consciously and deliberately. The idea that symbols and archetypal images generate observable changes in the human psyche lies at the heart of art therapy. This concept is the theoretical underpinning of the viability of expressive art practices as healing agents.[27] I will attempt to demonstrate this theory throughout this book with concrete examples of how working with symbols through masks has had a profound effect on my life.

Alchemy – Language of Transformation

Alchemy is a lost art whose usefulness has been rediscovered, in terms of depth psychology, by Carl Jung[28] and many notable, post-Jungian thinkers, such as Jeffrey Raff[29] and Edward Edinger.[30] Although the exact origins of alchemy are controversial, there are records of alchemy existing in ancient Arabia, Egypt, Greece, and China.[31] Alchemy is known as the art of transmutation, as its chief concern was transforming matter. The Western form of alchemy referenced by psychologists is European, or Latin alchemy which was an active art from 1100 to 1700 ad.[32] During the seventeenth and eighteenth centuries alchemy and its theories on matter and transformation were discredited by the newly emerging sciences of chemistry and physics.[33] The way medieval European alchemists described nature and the transformation of matter was convoluted and obtuse, which held no interest for the emerging scientific mind. Alchemy fell into obscurity for all but a handful of mystics and scholars.[34]

In the early twentieth century, Jung began to discover a profound link between alchemy and analytic psychology.[35] This inquiry opened when Richard Wilhelm sent Jung his translation of the alchemical Chinese Taoist text, *The Secret of the Golden Flower* in 1928.[36] Previously Jung had been frustrated by a flood of unconscious material for which he could find no known methods or systems of categorization which applied to his internal experience. Gnosticism provided some information, but the sources were very limited back then. Alchemical symbolism turned out to be the key Jung had been searching for. From reviewing the images, he deduced that in the process of trying to understand the mysteries of matter and transformation, the alchemists had projected onto matter the symbols and images of the unconscious.[37] Modern interest in alchemy as a symbolic language describing the psychological process of individuation is concerned with transformation of the personality.[38] Edward Edinger[39] describes the importance of alchemical symbolism to depth psychology:

> What makes alchemy so valuable for psychotherapy is that its images concretize the experiences of transformation that one undergoes in psychotherapy. Taken as a whole, alchemy provides a kind of anatomy of individuation. Its images will be most useful, of course, to those who have a personal experience of the unconscious.

At the heart of alchemy is the idea of the Philosopher's Stone, reputed to be a magical substance that held the power of transformation. Also known as the *lapis* or the alchemical gold, this stone was said to transmute metals, heal sickness, bestow its creator with immortality, and reveal the mysteries of spirit. In alchemy, every process and operation was centered on creating the Philosopher's Stone, which was the key to the ultimate mystery and magic of life. Jung saw a direct correlation between the Philosopher's Stone and his conception of the Self archetype, the symbol of unified wholeness.[40]

The stone begins in an undifferentiated state as a chaotic mix of the original substance, known as the *prima materia*, Latin, for *original matter*.[41] The *prima materia* is the indeterminate or chaotic state, the original matter that is there at the beginning of the process, both alchemically and psychologically.[42] This is an apt metaphor for the original state of the personal unconscious as an undifferentiated field of chaos, and also for the starting point of making any unconscious material conscious. The alchemist must subject the *prima materia* to certain operations in order to differentiate its component substances.

In individuation, this is the process of separating out the confusion of unconscious contents into its constituent parts. The components, in both cases, consist of various pairs of opposites. The final, most differentiated pair of opposites, represented in alchemical symbolism as the King and the Queen, is then united in the *coniunctio*, the mystical marriage. This union of opposites begets the powerfully transformative substance, the Philosopher's Stone. For Jung, this described the *transcendent function,* which is the union of opposing forces within the psyche which leads to a new, third way of being.[43]

The alchemical process requires containment in the form of the *vas hermetic,* or hermetic vessel. In psychology this can be anything that helps contain the transformation process including the therapeutic relationship, art, myths, ritual, and of course, masks. The first stage of the process is the *nigredo* (blackening) with its accompanying operations such as deconstruction, dismemberment, death, and decay. This is the mythological descent into darkness, the psychological death of rigid and limiting aspects of ego that must give way to the emergence of new aspects of personality aligned with the wisdom of the Self.[44] The *albedo* (whitening) is the phase of realization that comes after the *nigredo*, wherein new insights surface and spring to life from the fertilizing decay.[45] These first two stages of separation and purification lead up to, and eventually result in, the *coniunctio*, the union of opposites.

The final stage is the emergence of a new way of being, which follows the *coniunctio*. This phase is known as the *rubedo* (reddening) which is the successful completion that yields the *Lapis*.[46] Alchemical symbolism also parallels the stages of initiation, the narrative stages of myth, and the structure of ritual. The *nigredo*, is the death of the old way of being that comes with the separation. The *albedo* is the liminal phase where the transformation and resulting insights occur. The *rubedo* is the phase of return, where the initiate is re-aggregated into society and the hero returns with the treasure, with the gold.

Trickster – Archetype of Transformation

The Trickster is an ancient archetypal symbol found across times and cultures. Archetypes are, by their nature, hard to define and relegate to fixed, static definitions.[47] The Trickster is all the more challenging to describe because it is the embodiment of contradictions. The Trickster archetype represents the dualities and polarities that directly confront our desire for clarity, certainty, and stability. Trickster is unpredictable and has a pluralistic, shape-shifting nature that defies rigid structure. Trickster has long been associated with the mask due to the shape-shifting qualities of masks which transform the wearer while "tricking" the audience or viewer.

The Trickster is a liminal archetype associated with boundaries, edges, and places of transition.[48] It serves as a balancing agent, an equalizing force that challenges us to grow, oft-times employing discomfort to motivate the process along. Trickster is the character in myths and lore who stirs the pot, mixes things up, and brings a bit of chaos to an otherwise placid story.[49] Trickster is often the catalyst that pushes the storyline along by abruptly shifting the direction and because of this, is frequently the cause of distress. Trickster brings the unexpected and introduces the element of doubt into what was once certain. Trickster pokes holes in rigid boundaries and complicates situations with multiple points of view. It is the archetype that pushes us to question norms and to move beyond known limits. Trickster is involved any time we find ourselves examining assumptions or stretching ourselves in previously unexplored directions. It is that which stirs on the edges of thought and belief structures and thrusts us forward, as individuals and societies, into new frontiers.[50]

Because Trickster disrupts convention, it is commonly cast in a negative light. The Trickster is neither strictly positive nor negative – it is both and yet it is neither one. It expresses the paradox. Trickster is known to embody divine qualities while at the same time engaging in diabolical acts. It is hard to come to terms with something that is light and dark, good and bad, in and out, up and down, spirit and matter all at once. As humans, we struggle to grasp the possibility that unity can underlie apparent duality. Trickster is an amoral character who is not bound to standards and rules and so can contain and balance the paradoxes that often split and divide us humans - making it all the more tricky to define and apprehend.

In alchemy, the Trickster archetype manifests as the multifaceted and elusive symbol of *Mercurius*. Mercurius masterfully holds the duality of spirit in matter and is often associated with the *Lapis* – the Self, or unified whole. It is at once related to the Holy Trinity and paradoxically, to the devil. Carl Jung[51] said the following about Mercurius: "…his positive aspect relates him not only to the Holy Spirit, but in the form of the lapis, also to Christ, as a triad, even to the Trinity." He goes on to further illustrate this seemingly impossible contradiction: "In comparison with the purity and unity of the Christ symbol, Mercurius-lapis is ambiguous, dark, paradoxical and thoroughly pagan." He summarizes the conundrum nicely by stating," The paradoxical nature of Mercurius reflects an important aspect of the self – the fact, namely, that it is essentially a *complexion oppositorum*, and indeed can be nothing else if it is to represent any kind of totality."

In this way, the Trickster, in the form of the alchemical Mercurius, can be said to contain the totality of the psyche – both the unconscious and the conscious mind, the known and the unknown, and the light and dark within us all. Further, any symbol of divinity that attempts to encapsulate the entirety of creation must impartially encompass this dual nature or else fail to be complete and whole – which is itself a tricky concept to grasp. Jung[52] further illuminates the complexity of the Trickster archetype in the form of Mercurius:

> [I]t is not surprising that the spirit of Mercurius has, to say the least, a great many connections with the dark side. One of his aspects is the female serpent-daemon, Lilith or Melusina, who lives in the philosophical tree. At the same time, he not only partakes of the Holy Spirit but, according to alchemy, is actually identical with it. We have no choice but to accept this shocking paradox after all we have learnt about the ambivalence of the spirit archetype. Our ambiguous Mercurius simply confirms the rule.

Jung's description of the perplexing nature of Mercurius shows up in cross-cultural myths and stories of the Trickster archetype. Ananse the spider is a West African Trickster from the country of Ghana. He is a morally ambiguous character who fools humans and gods alike. His tricks are enhanced by his ability to change form and take whatever shape best suits his escapade. Yet some stories also cast him as divine creator who spun the entire world into being.[53]

The Greek god, Hermes is another famous example of a Trickster figure. He is a prankster and a thief as well as a beneficent creator who brought fire and music, among other things, to the human realm. Hermes is a border dweller that has the power to bridge the upper and lower worlds, and he is not bound to the laws of gods or men. He moves freely between the underworld, the human world, and the world of the gods and serves as messenger between the realms – making him an impeccable diplomat.[54] Trickster can cleverly show up in any guise and take the form of other archetypes, yet we can identify Trickster energy by the very nature of its changeability and its incendiary actions.

Trickster has been associated, by Jung and others, with the unconscious mind. Like the unconscious, the Trickster is unpredictable and beyond the conscious control of ego. From my research, I would say the Trickster is on the boundary, if there can be said to be one, between the conscious and the unconscious. The Trickster moves between the conscious and unconscious realms and can perhaps be viewed as a third condition - similar to the transcendent function in alchemy which unities the opposites and holds them in balance.

Trickster is a liminal archetype that lurks on the edges of transitional processes like initiation. In his book, *Thresholds of Initiation*, Joseph Henderson[55] describes the state of the uninitiated ego as existing in an archetypal Trickster cycle, a transitory state between youth and maturity. According to Henderson (1967), identification with the *puer aeternus,* the ego complex described earlier which is marked by stunted development and an adolescent fixation on the idea of eternal youth, often manifests as the Trickster archetype. It is the adult who has somehow failed to sufficiently grow up - an immature, yet tremendously powerful individual.

Internally, the Trickster archetype can be experienced as the split we have all encountered at one time or another. It is present in those times, situations, and relationships that give us mixed feelings in which we simultaneously experience love and hate, attraction and repulsion, joy and sorrow. It can also show up psychologically as doubt, which can be extremely uncomfortable yet growth promoting at the same time. Doubt is a precursor to change. James Hollis[56] addresses this in his book, *Swamplands of the Soul.*

> Given the fact that the top priority of the ego is security, doubt is an unwelcome visitor to us...*Doubt is the necessary fuel for change, and therefore growth.* There is no scientific or theological dogma which does not contain within it the seeds of reification and tyranny. Similarly, the psyche summons us, quite apart from the desires of the ego, to relinquish what seemed clear, what protected us, and thereby what now mires us in yesterday. The problem then is not doubt; the problem is fear of change. Confronting the risk of doubt is necessary for any group or individual to grow.

Certainty is the enemy of growth. Trickster, in the form of doubt, breaks us out of old categories in order to free our energy to flow into a new form. As an agent of change, Trickster triggers our fear of change and is an uneasy yet essential companion on the path of growth. Trickster is associated with the mask for several reasons including the shape-shifting qualities of masks and their ability to disguise and transform the identity of the wearer. The mask's ability to induce trance states is related to Trickster's ability to cross boundaries between the known and unknown. The Greek god Dionysus, along with being the god of music and of wine, is known to embody Trickster energy. Dionysus is also known as the god of the mask as well as the founder of ancient Greek theater, in which the mask was a primary tool.[57]

When the lens is focused on Trickster energy, it is easier to see its elusive movement and implications around us and within us. Everywhere there are references to the patterns the Trickster archetype portrays, perhaps because it embodies fundamental patterns of uncertainty that we fiercely struggle with and desperately need to reconcile within ourselves and our world.

Mask - Tool of Transformation

The mask is, in essence, a symbol of our ability to disguise and transform our basic identifying features. Masks conceal the identity of the wearer and are reputed to reveal deeper aspects of the personality that are typically hidden.[58] The absolute shift in appearance that is possible through wearing a mask has long been associated with the mystery of transformation. The mask is a Trickster-like medium used to explore boundaries and investigate the role of appearance in the experience of change.[59]

In his book *Masks, Transformation and Paradox,* A. David Napier[60] explores the relationship of masks to the concepts of paradox, ambiguity, and change. He posits that masks provide a means of investigating the problems posed by the paradoxical experiences that occur alongside transitional states. For example, an initiate can be simultaneously filled with longing and dread at the prospect of being isolated from their community during a rite of passage. An initiate may likewise feel insignificant and special at the same time. Similarly, a masked actor may experience the paradox of feeling like oneself and, at the same time, feeling like the character one is impersonating.

Napier[61] describes a paradox as "something that appears to be self-contradictory, a thing that at some time or from a particular point of view, appears to be what it is not." This concept is central to the art of masking. Paradoxes are by nature antinomies, in other words, unresolvable contradictions such as a mask wearer being at once self and other. Napier[62] explains:

> A paradox must by definition lead us at some time to perceive a contradiction, and in so doing necessitates an acceptance that things may look like what they are not. Our ability to accept this ambiguity is also fundamental to our recognition and signification of change. We know what things look like and recognize specific change because we are aware that something no longer is what it was... The special efficacy of masks in transformation results, perhaps, not only from the ability to address the ambiguities of point of view, but also from their capacity to elaborate what is

paradoxical about appearances and perceptions in the context of a changing viewpoint. Masks, that is, testify to an awareness of the ambiguities of appearance and to a tendency towards paradox characteristics of transitional states.

According to Napier, ambivalence is central to masking and masks tend to take on increased significance for cultures in which ambivalence is a central feature of their cosmologies, such as with the Greeks. Ambivalence is defined as continual fluctuation, uncertainty, and ambiguity.[63] A look at the Greek pantheon quickly reveals gods and goddesses that behave in contradictory fashion, depending on their ever-fluctuating moods. Changeability is at the heart of masking which is why masks are donned during times of personal and cultural transition. Transition brings uncertainty and paradoxical experiences and the ambiguous forces, spirits, and gods that inhabit the cosmos are invoked and appeased to ease the passage from one state to the next. Masks, by their very nature, convey paradox and ambiguity better than any other cultural artifact, making them the perfect art form to employ during the process of transformation.

In the next chapter, we're going to drop deeper into the nuts and bolts of the methods and techniques used in my personal work and my work with students to investigate the effects of masks on psychological experiences, particularly transformation.

End Notes

1. Victor and Edith Turner, 1978, p. 249
2. Hopcke, 1991; Turner & Turner, 1978
3. Turner & Turner, 1978
4. Hopcke, 1991; Turner & Turner, 1978
5. Turner & Turner, 1978
6. Turner & Turner, 1978, p. 3
7. Henderson, 1967; Mahdi, Foster, & Little, 1987
8. Henderson, 1967
9. Henderson, 1967
10. Henderson, 1967; Stein, 1998
11. Henderson, 1967; Stein, 1998
12. Henderson, 1967
13. Henderson, 1967, p.15
14. Henderson, 1967; Mahdi, et al. 1987
15. Henderson, 1967
16. Henderson, 1967
17. Schechner & Schuman, 1976
18. Henderson, 1967
19. Eck, 1981; Turner & Turner, 1978
20. Stevens, 1998
21. Stevens, 1998
22. Stevens, 1998, p. 26
23. Jung, 1977
24. Edinger, 1994
25. Jung, 1964
26. Henderson, 1967
27. McNiff, 2004
28. Jung, 1963
29. Raff, 2003
30. Edinger, 1995
31. Taylor, 1992
32. Raff, 2000; McLean, 1989
33. Henderson & Sherwood, 2003
34. Henderson & Sherwood, 2003
35. Henderson & Sherwood, 2003; Raff, 2000; McLean, 1989
36. Jung, 1963
37. Henderson & Sherwood, 2003
38. Raff, 2000
39. Edinger, 1991, p. 2
40. Edinger, 1991, 1995; Jung, 1964
41. Edinger, 1991
42. Edinger, 1991
43. Edinger, 1991, 1995; Swartz-Salant, 1995
44. Edinger,1991
45. Henderson & Sherwood, 2003

46. Henderson & Sherwood, 2003
47. Hyde, 1998
48. Hyde, 1998
49. Hyde, 1998
50. Hyde, 1998
51. Jung, 1967, p. 241
52. Jung, 1967, p. 240
53. Christen 1998; Allen & Phillips, 2000
54. Christen 1998; Allen & Phillips, 2000
55. Henderson, 1967
56. Hollis, 1996, p. 56
57. Kerenyi, 1976
58. Nunley & McCarty, 1999
59. Napier, 1986
60. Napier, 1986
61. Napier, 1986, p. 1
62. Napier, 1986, p. 1
63. Merriam-Webster, 1973

5 EXPLORING PSYCHE

Before we look at the mechanics of depth-oriented mask work, it's important to have a broader understanding of how to approach and work with the unconscious. It can be tricky business and should not be approached without the proper understanding, tools to contain it, and a support system to help you if you get stuck or overwhelmed. The unconscious is a powerful field of energy and when it erupts into consciousness it can be rattling to the ego. This is why we approach it gently, through tried and true techniques such as art therapy and somatic therapies (working with the body).

People often do not approach the unconscious voluntarily. They become aware of it when they have collisions with it or experience some type of crisis. This can best be described as those inexplicable inner conflicts that we can't seem to resolve. For example, think of a time when you've become aware of urges in yourself that seem irrational, primitive, destructive, or totally at odds with your conscious opinions and attitudes. It can be unsettling and confusing. Yet, as they persist, and if they are not handled, they can develop into a neurosis. Typically, neuroses afflict us when our conscious attitudes contradict our deeper, instinctual selves. When psychological symptoms such as depression or anxiety emerge which demand our attention, we then begin to feel the very real impact of the unconscious acting itself out in our daily lives. This is often when we start to realize we need to work with the unconscious in order to address the internal imbalances that have led to our suffering.

The heart of the mask work I engage in involves using masks in combination with depth psychology and art therapy methods, (described in the following chapters), to come into a more conscious relationship with hidden aspects of the psyche. I use a variety of techniques to explore the interior archetypal drama and to give form and structure to mercurial inner processes. My work has been guided by several different methodologies from which I have drawn inspiration and techniques to deepen the experience. My work has been strongly influenced by Heuristic Inquiry, Depth Inquiry, and Art-Based Research. A brief look into these methods will help create a clearer picture of my particular approach to masks. I explain and define each method one by one throughout the next three chapters and elucidate the overall scope of foraying into the inner world via symbolic mask work.

When approaching this type of creative self-awareness work, I tell my students to think of the work as being an investigation or a research project focused on their own psyche. I ask them to imagine that they're detectives, tracking and recording clues to later be pieced together to solve a mystery. That's essentially what we're doing in this work. We're diving into the mystery of our inner selves and with perseverance and a bit of luck, bringing back a treasure trove of insight and wisdom.

Heuristic Research and the Lived Experience

The developments that unfolded as I spent several years doing in-depth mask explorations were guided primarily by my own inner process and my work with the masks. However, my research experience also happened to map onto the Heuristic Research model quite effectively. Heuristic Inquiry, developed by Clark Moustakas[1], is a qualitative research method which is particularly suited to psychological studies. This is because it takes into account the frame of reference and personal involvement of the researcher. Heuristic Inquiry centralizes around the *lived experience* of the researcher and the transformations that occur for the researcher during (and as a result of) the course of an investigation. This is what we're doing with mask work; we are directly experiencing and being transformed by our exploration or research into psyche.

In the heuristic method, the research question emerges from a deeply personal origin and prompts a process of inner discovery that requires participation, deep engagement, and the ability to surrender to uncertainty and unpredictability. The word heuristic is derived from the Greek word *heuriskein*, meaning *to find* or *to discover*.

Heuristic research is about comprehensively exploring a question in order to get at the essence and meaning of the experience investigated - which can be a difficult task. It takes a tremendous amount of focus and perseverance to conduct a depth psychological inquiry. This work is not for the dabbler. It is an unusually demanding form of research that requires the investigator to be involved in the inquiry on every level. This form of research engages more than the ego. It reaches to the depths of one's being to unearth unconscious wounds and complexes, ultimately leading to authentic psychological transformation on the part of the researcher.[2] Which is why this model of investigation is so well suited to depth-oriented mask work.

In Moustakas' words[3]; "Through exploratory open-ended inquiry, self-directed search, and immersion in active experience, one is able to get inside the question, become one with it, and thus achieve an understanding of it." Human experience contains phenomena which are challenging to track and understand, let alone describe within the limits of verbal language. It is these areas of understanding which are often addressed in heuristic research. Self-inquiry is used to discover and illuminate the essence of important human experiences through the lens of an individual with the hopes of contributing to our larger understanding of the individual and the greater human experience.

Heuristic research is divided into six stages, summarized very briefly below. It encompasses alternative ways of knowing such as *intuition* and *tacit knowing* applied to domains such as inspiration, dreams, images, and reflection - all of which are important aspects of inquiry into psyche. Tacit knowing is linked to the experience of revelation and can be described as an inherent, implicit knowing.[4] For example, we can recognize the face or voice of a loved one and have the ability to pick out that single face or voice from millions while being unable to describe or articulate the mechanism through which we are able to do this. We recognize the face without fundamentally knowing *how* we know or without being able to clearly describe the unmistakable sense of "knowing" experienced. It is the experience of simply knowing something without knowing how we know it.[5]

Intuition

Intuition makes it possible to perceive something as a whole from viewing the parts, and it allows one to make inferences that lead to unified understanding. Intuition is an experience of immediate knowledge that lies outside of the faculties of reason and logic. It is the great and mysterious power that leads to unprecedented ideas and surprising originality.[6] Intuition forms a bridge linking the implicit knowing of tacit knowledge to explicit knowledge which can be directly observed and described.[7] The use of intuition and tacit knowing is central to ritual mask work, as is a heuristic approach to understanding the material elucidated by working with masks.

The Six Stages of Heuristic Inquiry

Stage One: Initial Engagement

The task at this preliminary stage is to identify a topic or question of passionate interest that holds both personal meaning and social significance. In terms of masking, it's a question that we have a burning desire to answer and normal modes of questioning have not been able to adequately reveal the answer. For example, I have struggled with something along the lines of, "What is blocking me from sharing my creative work that explores the phenomenon of psychic wounding?" Or, "Why am I so inexplicably captivated by mask work?" I entered the masking project I describe in this book with the burning question: "What or whom is the 'spirit of the mask,' the mysterious 'other' that seems to appear when a mask is donned?"

The entire heuristic research process emerges from the discovery of a question so compelling that it has the power to initiate deep and sustained inquiry. This is really important. It takes a deep passion and 'need to know' to sustain this type of inquiry all the way through to yield the desired results of fully illuminating a piece of shadow material. When embarking on a masking exploration, it can be helpful to have a focused question in mind, even if it is more general in nature, such as to learn more about a shadow area of your life or to explore a particular complex that you struggle with. For me, the deeper mask inquiries occurred when I first encountered the presence of another, separate personality while wearing a mask. I was immediately captivated.

The masking experiences I had early on in the psychology master's program ignited an immediate fascination and curiosity which plunged me into a survey of the history and use of masks. It became the topic I could not put out of my mind. It seemed to follow me everywhere. It was as if the mask had me in its grips and was not going to let me go until I gave it due recognition. I can only describe it as the feeling that the topic chose me. When something in our psyche needs to be addressed and worked with, I have found that it makes itself known, though often in an obscure and symbolic way. It's our intuition and tacit knowing that guide us into the inquiry in the first place.

Stage Two: Immersion

In this phase the question is more clearly defined and the researcher/explorer literally becomes immersed in living with the question. She enters into the topic through every available avenue and remains alert to every place and every way the theme presents itself in waking and dreaming life. Moustakas[8] describes the attitude of this phase as one of "sustained focus and concentration." Virtually any avenue - books, film, nature, conversations, conferences, performances - can offer insight into the phenomenon being investigated. Synchronicities and dreams can play an important role in bringing related material up from the unconscious to be integrated into the investigation. I'll talk more about working with synchronicities in Chapter Six.

Stage Three: Incubation

Here we step away from intense external focus on the question or topic – the creating, ritualizing, reading, researching, and talking about it. Active participation is withdrawn so that the deep inner dimension of tacit knowing is able to inform the inquiry. During this time growth and development is taking place on an inner, intuitive level. Moustakas[9] describes the nature of incubation, "[A] seed has been planted, the seed undergoes silent nourishment, support and care that produces a creative awareness of some dimension of phenomenon or a creative integration of its parts or qualities." At this stage it is necessary for the researcher to let go and trust that the process is progressing on deeper, unseen levels, like a seed germinating in the earth. A seed will push up in its own time. Natural development cannot be rushed.

Stage Four: Illumination

The illumination process is characterized by the awakening of new insights and new dimensions of knowledge and understanding. It's an organic result of taking time to incubate. This part of the process emerges naturally when one is open to tacit knowing and intuition. Moustakas describes it as a breakthrough of information and clarity into conscious awareness. It is a time of creative discovery that requires receptivity and active reflection on the part of the explorer (similar to the albedo phase in alchemy).

Stage Five: Explication

In this stage the researcher works to comprehensively examine the newly awakened insights with concentrated focus. Here, additional angles and features are elucidated and refinements and corrections are made. In this phase a thorough delineation of the dominant themes is fully developed.[10] This will all become clearer as you read the coming chapters, but here's an example to help illustrate this idea. In my own process it went like this: in the summer of 2012, all of the experiences and research I had been doing with masks for the previous three years began to weave together into a clear picture.

Suddenly I began to understand that the masks I had created and was working with were, in fact, guiding me through an initiation process. I hadn't realized it while I was in the immersed in the work. It was as if, suddenly, all of these disparate areas of interest and pieces of data began coalescing into a unified understanding of the true scope of my work with the masks. It was incredibly exciting to see the massive amounts of material I had collected begin coming together after months of overwhelm and confusion. Finally it all started to gel.

Stage Six: Creative Synthesis

This final phase of a heuristic investigation is entered once the researcher has thoroughly familiarized herself with the topic and has achieved a level of mastery of the material investigated. At this point, tacit knowing and intuition come into play once again. The explorer enters a period of solitude in order to contemplate the knowledge and data acquired. The topic and questions are meditated upon with concentrated focus so that the inspiration necessary for true creative synthesis can emerge.

The goal at this stage is to pull all of the components and core themes into a synergized whole that can be communicated to others through any means: narrative, poetry, painting, performance, or other creative forms. Like with all phases of heuristic inquiry, creative synthesis cannot be forced and comes in its own time and only after the previous stages have been successfully completed.

After nearly three years of engaging in mask work, coupled with numerous pivotal spiritual encounters including a wilderness vision fast; immersion in the ancient Chinese art of qigong; and work with an African shaman, I reached a point in the summer of 2012 where I knew it was time to synergize and articulate my experiences.

I spent three months in relative solitude, focusing intently on all of the accumulated materials and experiences I had with the three masks I describe later in the book. Then after four days of sitting silently in nature with my husband I returned home with renewed energy and an inscrutable determination to write my master's thesis, from which this book is derived. With inexplicable clarity, I sat down at my computer and wrote out almost the entire document in four feverishly focused weeks. I finally saw the links between the masks I had created and was working with and the process of my own psychological initiation which had been contained and guided by them.

This gives you an overview of the steps involved in conducting a depth-oriented inquiry into psyche – which is what we're doing with ritual mask work. In the next chapter, I explain the specific techniques used to deepen into this level of mask work in order to yield the levels of transformation I allude to.

End Notes

1. Moustakas, 1990
2. Coppin & Nelson, 2005
3. Moustakas, 1990, p.15
4. Moustakas, 1990
5. Moustakas, 1990
6. Polanyi, as cited in Moustakas, 1990
7. Moustakas, 1990
8. Moustakas, 1990, p. 28
9. Moustakas, 1990, p. 29
10. Moustakas, 1990

6 GATHERING TOOLS

Now we are ready to get into the specific methods and tools I use in my personal mask work and in working with students. As you can see already, there are numerous components and layers of understanding necessary to facilitate depth-oriented mask work. That said, I have found that students with minimal knowledge of the human psyche and the psychology of transformation can benefit greatly from this work. However, I believe this background knowledge is essential for those who wish to guide others into this powerful form of mask work.

Depth Inquiry

Depth inquiry includes methods such as active imagination, visual art methods (collage, painting, drawing), authentic movement, tracking synchronicities, and immersion in nature. These methods have all been an important part of my work with masks, particularly in the early phases of creating the masks and generating the ritual performance.

Active Imagination

Active imagination is a method developed by Jung to engage the non-ordinary state of the imaginal realm, as discussed in Chapter Two. Active imagination involves two stages: the first is letting the unconscious come forward; the second involves interacting with the unconscious material in order to assimilate it. Jung emphasized the power and value of this method in integrating and shifting unconscious material. Throughout his career he advocated for the recognition of the inestimable importance of imagination in the development of the individual as well as human culture.[1]

One enters an active imagination by relaxing into an alert yet receptive state and allowing the raw material of the unconscious to emerge in the form of images, symbols, emotions, or impulses.[2] Or one can choose an image from a dream, vision or reverie and concentrate on it with focused attention, allowing the faculty of imagination to take hold. It is important to note that the ego participates and asserts its views when interacting with the unconscious material, but it does not manipulate or control what takes place.[3] The ego participates with curiosity, openness, and sincerity; treating the images and figures of the inner world as real people and interacting with them as if they are separate from oneself (because they are separate from the ego).

Because it is an interaction with something beyond ego consciousness, the outcome of a true active imagination is always unknown.[4] It is an active interface with the unconscious (as opposed to a passive fantasy); it is focused and engages emotional states. Robert Johnson[5] explains that the experience itself is therapeutic. Even if the analytical mind never is fully able to understand or interpret the active imagination, it still changes a person on deep, inner levels and observably shifts behaviors and attitudes. Much of the work in this book derives its potency from the use of active imagination. (You will see examples of active imagination dialogues in later chapters and in the appendices).

Movement

A number of movement based methods have been developed for use in psychotherapy. *Authentic Movement* is one such innovative method designed to merge creative, psychological and sacred dimensions together in a body centered process.[6] Developed by Mary Starks Whitehouse, it is based on active imagination, and is designed to enhance symbolic exploration through physical movement and expression. Starks posits that acting out emotions and impulses through the body leads to deeper understanding and integration than is accessed through other forms of expression.[7] The practice itself involves improvisational and spontaneous movement that is performed free of direction and expectation, allowing the mover to explore psychological processes from a kinesthetic perspective. Engaging in somatic exploration of psychic material is particularly powerful and transformative. Robert Johnson[8] explains the power of physical action:

> Doing a physical act has a magical effect...setting up a connection between the conscious mind and the unconscious, sending a powerful message back to the unconscious causing changes to take place at the deep levels where our attitudes and values originate.

This method of creating masked rituals is not an abstract or theoretical experience. It is grounded and embodied in physical form, requiring the engagement of body as well as psyche and spirit. Movement is an intrinsic part of working with masks.

Synchronicities

Jung[9] coined the term synchronicity to express his concepts about acausal connections between phenomena. He wrote an entire book on the subject, *Synchronicity: An Acausal Connecting Principle,* from which the following information has been taken, unless otherwise noted.

The idea of synchronicity was formulated from his observation of coincidence as it appeared in his life and that of his patients. The coincidences he observed were not senseless or simple coincidences; they held significant meaning for the person experiencing them. Thus, a synchronicity is about significant coincidence where two or more events occur that are causally unrelated yet are experienced as occurring together in a meaningful way. The theory rests on Jung's theory of the archetypes; synchronicities occur around archetypal symbols.[10]

The well-known example of such a meaningful coincidence is given in Jung's story of his work with a patient who had reached an impasse in her therapy. One night the patient dreamt of a golden scarab beetle. The next day, during her therapy session, a golden beetle flew into the room. Jung caught it and was able to identify it as a golden scarab, which was not known to exist in the alpine environment of Switzerland. When Jung examined the symbolism of the golden beetle, it rendered viable information that helped his patient progress in her therapy.

I have personally observed and recorded synchronicities long before I knew about Jung's theory. It's been a particularly interesting phenomenon that has piqued my curiosity as long as I can remember. I think of it as a meeting of our inner world with the outer world in a mysterious, almost magical way. Noting synchronicities is a part of my work with masks. I share several synchronicities that occurred throughout the course of this project, in later chapters, to give you a more concrete idea of how this works together, in the context of ritual mask work, to form a more full and illuminating experience.

Visual Art

Working with art as a method for deep inquiry into psyche involves four phases, as explained by Jill Mellick[11] in her book *The Natural Artistry of Dreams*. It begins with Intentional departure from ordinary awareness; moves into an inner journey into the imagination; followed by a return to ordinary awareness; and culminates in reflection on the journey. Following these phases helps encourage material to be communicated across the boundaries of the unconscious mind in a way that the information can be integrated into conscious awareness. The first and last phases are key components of integrated creativity and distinguish it from ordinary art-making processes.

Expressive art which is intended to inform the creator and help integrate personal material into conscious awareness, like all of this work, requires creating the right time, the right place, and the right state of mind. The more relaxed and contemplative a person is, the higher the probability of deep insight and integration. It is important to bring full attention to the process. It is important to give the imagination room for unfettered expression without interruptions and outside influences.

It is essential to let go of the need for exact outcomes, particularly excellence, performance, or specific content. This type of creative work requires detachment from goals.[12] While our conscious minds have reasons for engaging in this work, our unconscious has deeper information for us. If we are attached to our conscious intentions, we can miss the real gems of the experience. It is important to release expectations about the product and immerse fully into the process, letting go of desires to later interpret, praise or criticize. Ideally the whole process is uncensored and spontaneous.

There is a large body of work on the healing efficacy of the arts, and a survey of the material is well beyond the scope of this book, however it bears mentioning briefly. In his book, *The Archetypal Imagination*, psychologist James Hollis[13] gives several examples of how engaging in art practices has eased the suffering and contributed to the overall quality of life for patients suffering from trauma and terminal illnesses. He discusses evidence of art-based methods working to change the physiology of the brain. He gives powerful examples as follows:

> Studies at Baylor College of Medicine have indicated that when children are traumatized, critical pathways of the brain are arrested, leading to intellectual and emotional impairment. A growing body of evidence suggests that the expressive arts seem to reactivate those portions of the brain and reinstitute growth. Moreover, a study out of Stanford University indicated that the expressive arts are more efficacious than other interventions...

For me, art has always been a tool for self-expression and self-understanding. It has provided a way to take often conflicting and overwhelming thoughts, feelings, and experiences and put them outside of myself, onto a canvas or paper, for example. Once it is outside, I can begin digesting it, assimilating it, taking it back in in an integrated way. Art has helped me to process my thoughts and emotions and to heal from trauma, and I have seen it have this effect on others as well.

Art-based Methods

Art-based research is defined as the use of artistic processes as the primary means of examining and understanding an experience.[14] Art-based research includes important methods such as dialoging with images and interpreting images as a way to deepen one's understanding of the material being examined.

Dialoguing with Images

Dialoguing with images is a process similar to active imagination and is an art therapy method that has been informed by Jung's work with the imagination. Prominent Art Therapist Shaun McNiff describes art therapy as a therapy of the imagination that is centered on establishing a relationship through dialogue with the "imaginal other" present in the art. Just as in active imagination, the ego interacts with the figures and symbols that emerge in the art-making process in order to learn about their nature and purpose. McNiff[15] delineates this approach to working with art: "This therapeutic perspective, or drama, experiences depth and meaning by staying with the characters of imagination, letting them speak, reveal themselves, and emerge according to their respective nature."

Through these types of interaction with art objects, one can gain insight into the contents of the unconscious. I combine this method with active imagination and have found it to be tremendously revealing. As you will see in the coming chapters, I have been able to uncover deeply buried unconscious material by creating pieces of art and then contemplating and dialoguing with them to unpack the meaning they hold for me. I have also done this work frequently with students with great results.

Interpreting Images

Interpreting images is a helpful way to uncover psychological meaning in art. McNiff[16] advises to keep in mind that any interpretation of a piece of art contains the projections of the interpreter and reveals their unique perspective and fixations. Effective interpretations remain fluid and flexible and do not reify a work or limit it to a rigid explanation. An interpretation is not so much an explanation, but a method for opening up associations, free-form thoughts, and emotions in the viewer. It is a way of deepening the relationship one has to an art piece. Interpretation can have a deeply healing effect on psyche when done correctly.[17] Meaning emerges through the use of imagination, rather than rational thinking, and comes from deep within the psyche.

End Notes

1. Chodorow, 1997
2. Chodorow, 1997; Johnson, 1986
3. Johnson, 1986
4. Jung, 1997
5. Johnson, 1986
6. Adler, 2002
7. Adler, 2002
8. Johnson, 1986, p. 99
9. Jung, 1955
10. Coombs & Holland, 1990; Jung, 1955
11. Mellick, 1996
12. Malchiodi, 2002; McNiff, 2004; Mellick, 1996
13. Hollis, 2000, p. 9
14. McNiff, 1998
15. McNiff , 2004, p. 86
16. McNiff , 2004
17. Malchiodi, 2002; McNiff 2004

7 EMBARKING ON THE JOURNEY

The Masking Process

There are two major steps in the process of creating the masked ritual, each one containing a number of phases. The first, is the creation of the mask. The second is designing and executing the masked ritual performance. These two down into roughly seven phases.

The seven basic steps of creating the masked ritual are:

> 1) Identifying the archetypal symbol
> 2) Investigating its movement in psyche through active imagination and expressive arts
> 3) Exploring the archetype through cross-cultural amplification
> 4) Creating the mask
> 5) Setting the ritual container
> 6) Doing the ritual performance
> 7) Reflecting on the process

Given the mercurial nature of this type of work, I have found that the above stages contravened discrete boundaries, overlapping and altering order according to the dictates of psyche. For example, sometimes I have a symbol or archetype in mind before I create a mask. At others times, I make the mask first and then see what symbols and archetypes emerge from it. Both ways are valid and effective. For me, it seems to occur in different ways according to the needs of my psyche at any given moment.

I use a combination of my intuition and my intellect to decide which approach to take. If I have a symbol that's been coming up and I want to understand it better and illuminate it further, then I'll begin with a symbol. If I have vague and amorphous feelings and psychic stirrings that I cannot pinpoint, yet am feeling disturbed by, I may create a mask first and then see what archetypes and symbols seem to constellate around it. I give examples of several approaches later in the book. For the sake of clarity, I'll describe the steps in the order noted above, re-emphasizing that they may not occur in this order when one actually engages in the work.

Creating the mask

As mentioned above, you can begin the work in the order that best suits your particular needs at any given moment. You may have an inner experience trying to make itself known through what I refer to as the "itchy-scratchies" - those uncomfortable, mercurial stirrings that make you feel somehow out of whack or "off." If that's your starting point, I suggest you go right into creating a mask, following intuitive hunches and impulses. Once the mask is completed, you can engage in imaginal processes, outlined throughout this book, to learn more about it. This approach will be illustrated further in Chapter Seventeen with my work with the Horned One mask.

Identifying Archetypes and Symbols

Another effective approach is to enter the initial stage of mask work by looking for recurring archetypes and symbols in dreams, in reverie states, in synchronicities, in any of your creative work such as art of any kind, through free-writing and intuitive impulses that seem to come directly from the unconscious. As you move through daily life, watch for clues to help you understand what your psyche is oriented toward at a particular time.

Play Detective

In environments and interactions start paying attention to things like:

- What are you attracted to?
- What draws your attention?
- Where does your focus go?
- What excites and inspires you?
- What makes you uncomfortable?
- What distracts or repels you?

Record the Clues

I have found it helpful to record all of the above phenomena and observations in my personal journal using words, colors and images to try and capture the essence of each experience. I then am able to examine my reflections for persistent patterns that circle a particular archetypal motif. I typically notice that several archetypal themes are active in my psyche at any given time. I find it important to attend to all of the archetypes and symbols present but others may prefer to isolate, as best they can, and work with one at a time.

I have tried to isolate and found it to never break down quite that simply and neatly, but you may have a different experience. For me, even when I try to work with just one symbol or archetype, they seem to be in an important dynamic relationship with other archetypes and symbols. I have found that to understand the way an individual archetype shows up in my daily life, it helps to understand its relationships to other aspects of my psyche. In addressing a collection of archetypes vying for my attention, I am often able to see how they connect and interrelate in my internal and external realities.

At any rate, it is essential to record your observations of yourself – feelings, thoughts, dreams, your environment and synchonicities, and any "stirring" interactions you have with others. It doesn't have to be a detailed or time consuming process. If you're pressed for time, jotting down key words and phrases that will jog your memery later can be enough. What you're doing is trying to capture all of the clues inside and around you that will later inform your understanding of the unconscious material as it surfaces. If this seems confusing, don't worry. It will become more clear as you read the coming chapters with explicit examples of this work in action.

Amplifying Archetypes and Symbols

Once I have identified the archetype or symbol I want to work with, I begin exploring it through the techniques described in the previous chapter, such as active imagination and various forms of expressive art including drawing, painting, collage, sculpting, authentic movement, and poetry. I begin by trying to identify my personal associations with the archetype/symbol by asking questions such as:

- What or who or when does this remind me of?
- What associations do I have with this archetype/symbol?
- How do I feel about this archetype/symbol?

Then I engage in a process known as *archetypal amplification* which involves conducting research on how and where the symbol or archetype has appeared throughout various time periods and cultures. I gather information on it through as many avenues as possible. Once I have a more global picture of the archetype, I see what aspects of the archetypal stories and images feel most relevant for me at the time of investigation. I also keep in mind the larger scope of qualities and characteristics of the archetype, knowing that sometimes the things that I am initially oblivious to, or even repulsed by, can end up being the most powerful features of my work with it. So here's a breakdown of things you're looking for:

- When and where has this archetype/symbol appeared in the past?
- What's been said about this archetype/symbol?
- What stories and myths are connect to this archetype/symbol?
- How has it shown up for me, in my life?
- What characteristics or qualities of this archetype/symbol intrigue me or "speak to me"?

- How does my personal story relate to what I've learned about this archetype/symbol?

How to Get Started

Decide

I may work with anywhere from three to more than a dozen archetypal symbols or motifs at any one time. So, how do I decide which ones to create masks for? The first impulse to create a mask usually comes during meditation or trance journey work or when I immerse myself fully in nature. I will get a clear vision of a mask while my mind is in a relaxed, receptive, and creative state (see p.29 for a definition of a creative state). I recommend using techniques, like those mentioned above, to get really present in the body and in the here and now. Then, ask a question and listen within for the answer. I typically find that the first thought is the best thought, as it is more likely to come directly from the unconscious and bypasses ego editing, as demonstrated by its immediacy. So I get into a creative state and ask myself a question. I listen deep inside for the answer and have found it best to trust the first thing that comes. I make sure to record this in my journal so I can refer back to it as needed.

Act and Allow

Although the initial inspiration for the mask comes while I am in an altered state of consciousness, the mask itself seems to take on a form of its own during the process of creation. The vision is like an acorn seed. I never know what the finished product, the "tree," will look like when it is grown. As I create the mask, I set out with the initial idea in mind, but I find that the mask shapes itself as I go. I engage in active imagination with the raw materials of the mask and allow it to guide me in every step of the creative process. I rely heavily on the faculty of intuition when doing this work.

As this is not a handbook on mask-making, I will not go into to detailed descriptions on the process of creating masks. There are many materials and processes that can be used, and a survey of them is beyond the scope of this book. For folks who want more guidance in this area, you can find resources on my website: AlembicArts.com.

The key to the depth mask work I engage in is staying centered around working with the unconscious. Throughout the process of creating the mask, I pay attention to the places and ways the archetype or symbol continues showing up in my waking and dreaming life. This adds to the richness of understanding I am able to derive from my work with masks.

Stay Open and Flexible

Part of the magic of this work is that you never know what you're going to get. You may start with what you think is a clear idea of the mask you're going to create and work with, only to find that it completely changes over the course of your work with. I advise all who want to approach this work to let the process truly be *creative*. Let go and let the unexpected come forward. If what you end up with is in some way surprising, then you're on the right path. This is how you know it is unconscious content and not just your ego going after what it desires. Start with the unknown and let it develop moment by moment - that is where the mystery and magic is.

For myself, I have noted that the Trickster archetype is always at play in my work. Sometimes I think I am creating a mask for a particular archetype, but when it is finished and I begin working with it, it turns out to be a different one altogether. I have to remain flexible and open to the mystery.

Designing the Ritual and Performance

When the mask is complete, or sometimes while I am still working on it, I begin thinking about the ritual process. Like masking, engaging in rituals is an ancient and ubiquitous practice. People have created and participated in rituals since the dawn of human culture. Our prehistoric ancestors used ritual to make contact with the inner world. It was an effortless extension of psychic life connected with dreaming, myth-making, and the impulse towards creative expression. In his writings, Jung spoke of ritual and ceremony as essential pathways to the unconscious. Ritual is an innate human faculty, similar to dreaming, which allows communication to occur between the conscious mind and the unconscious.[1]

Ritual

Author and Jungian analyst, Robert Johnson[2] says of ritual, "At its best, ritual is a series of physical acts that expresses in condensed form one's relationship to the inner world of the unconscious." The function of ritual in the development of consciousness has to do with its ability to transform symbolic encounters into physical and concrete experiences. Understanding symbols intellectually is helpful, but when we can experience the power of a symbol emotionally and physically in our bodies, the depth and breadth of its meaning expands and deepens considerably. When our understanding of a symbol remains purely at the level of mind it is easier to detach from the essential qualities of a symbol which lie beyond the faculty of intellect and touch upon feeling states and even spiritual experiences. Johnson[3] goes on to say "...if we do something to express the symbol- something that involves our bodies and our emotions – the symbol becomes a living reality for us. It etches itself indelibly on our consciousness."

Ritual is a helpful tool in elucidating the quintessence of a symbol, of an archetypal energy, reducing the intensity of the primordial forces enough so that we can convert them into immediate, felt experiences.[4] Ritual brings these immense energies of the collective unconscious down to a human scale so that we can work with them and assimilate them into our conscious awareness. Through the ritual act, we are able to bring the archetype or symbol into the concrete physical dimension and integrate it into our daily lives.

Historically, masks have been associated with culturally defined rituals which involve the community. The ritual practices I engage in and refer to in this book are personal, individual rituals created around my personal process. In the hybrid American society I was born into we no longer have culturally established rituals to turn to. Yet we can each go within, into our own imaginations, to find the rituals that will reconnect us to our deeper selves, to the personal and collective unconscious manifest in each of our psyches. Rituals now must be custom made out of the raw material of the inner terrain.[5] The inspiration and impulse to create a ritual comes from the same place as dreams and intuitive art. Ritual emerges from and is connected to the same deep inner well of creativity, and therefore all of these means of expression work together and support each other.

The Components of Ritual

For me, ritual begins with setting an intention for the experience. In the work I describe in this book, my intention is typically as simple as connecting to the essence, the spirit, or archetypal presence of whichever mask I am working with in the ritual. The next task is setting aside a designated time and creating a special, sacred space in which to hold the ritual. Again, I like to keep this step simple and accessible. I find that rituals do not need to be extensive or elaborate in order to be effective. I usually set aside thirty minutes to an hour in a private space where I can be alone and undisturbed, such as my bedroom. Creating the time, the space, and the intention is the way in which I set a psychic container and send a message to my unconscious that I am preparing the way for deep material to enter into my waking reality.

Once alone in my space, I do a simple visualization to ground my awareness into my body and into the body of the Earth. I do a symbolic cleansing with incense, water, feathers, or tones from chimes or bowls, depending on the nature of the ritual I am performing. I then create an imaginal circle or container, demarcating a non-ordinary time and space. I cross my imaginary threshold and enter the circle, the mythic realm, being mindful to remain present, open to the experiences that take place and alert to changes in my physical, emotional and mental state.

Masked Rituals

In masking rituals, I then invoke the spirit of the mask with a simple phrase, such as "Spirit of the mask, I invite you to move and speak through me." I put the mask over my face, close my eyes, take several deep breaths and wait to feel a shift in my body and my consciousness. This is a process is similar to a technique used in theatrical mask work known as *dropping in*. Eli Simon,[6] in his book *Masking Unmasked: Four Approaches to Basic Acting*, gives a thorough description of how one goes about inhabiting a mask, including the method of dropping in, which I will explain shortly. First, I want to share the following quotes to reinforce the mystery and power of mask work:

> Masking promotes a comprehensive inhabitation of another being. This includes physical, emotional, vocal, and psychological transformation. You breathe new air. See with new eyes. Think new thoughts. Experience new needs...Masks are simple objects that cover your face. Yet they are capable of instigating transformative experiences...With practice and patience masking often seems like dreaming.[7]

Dropping In

Simon recommends that the mask actor (wearer) begin with certain prerequisite states of mind, including openness, positivity, focus, and curiosity. He describes helpful warm up activities to prepare for dropping in to the trance-like state induced by masks. These activities are based on simple body-mind techniques such as: relaxing the body and standing in a neutral position where the body is aligned and centered; engaging in controlled, relaxed breathing; shaking out tension and loosening limbs; relaxing vocal chords with sustained vowel sounds, much like the yogic practice of Om-ing.

After warming up, the process of dropping in begins. Remaining alert, relaxed, and physically and emotionally neutral, the mask actor puts the mask on. Attending to breath, the actor becomes fully present in the moment, opening to whatever comes while resisting the desire to push the experience in a particular direction.

Contact with the "Other"

Once the transformation begins and the presence of the other is experienced, the actor begins to slowly move according to the guidance and impulses that arise directly from the mask. This all may sound very abstract to a person who has not had the experience; yet to anyone who has inhabited a mask, and many have, the experience is as real as it is clear. I can feel when a masked being enters and departs. I attempt to illustrate the experience in detail in the chapters that follow.

Inhabiting the Mask

After I feel the presence of the other, achieved through the techniques described above, I then allow myself to spontaneously move and speak unedited according to impulses that arise. I let this go on until it reaches its own natural crescendo and the energy driving the experience subsides. I find that rituals, like any work of art, reach their own natural conclusion point and I have a clear intuitive sense of when a work is complete.

Returning and Recording

At that point, I take off the mask, offer my gratitude to the spirit or archetype and to my own psyche, and then I cross back over the imaginal threshold, dissolve the container and return to my ordinary world. Immediately after the experience, I record it in my journal and reflect upon the experience as a whole. I feel that this is a crucial step in terms of beginning to understand and integrate the experiences that take place within the ritual.

In summary, I find that the properties of the masked ritual work that has unfolded from my research is comprised of seven basic steps – identifying the archetypal symbol; engaging with it through active imagination and expressive arts; exploring the archetype or symbol further through amplification; creating the mask; setting the ritual container; performing the ritual; and then reflecting on it. Though it's important to note that the steps do not necessarily occur in the order they've been listed. Sometimes they do. Then again, sometimes they do not.

In the next several chapters, I take you on the journey with me through the step-by-step processes that evolved from my work with masks. I illuminate stages of my journey with the masks by exploring the creation, the rituals, and the insights gained through working with each mask in a series of three. But first, I present an overview of the levels of masking, as I've experienced them, to help you understand where my work with each mask fits into the continuum of masking practices I've uncovered through my experiential investigations.

End Notes

1. Johnson, 1986
2. Johnson, 1986, p. 103
3. Johnson, 1986, p. 103
4. Gendlin, 1986; Johnson, 1986
5. Johnson, 1986
6. Simon, 2003
7. Simon, 2003, p. 2

8 LAYERS AND LEVELS

Here's a brief overview of what I set out looking for and what I discovered on my journey with the three masks I'm about to introduce you to. I began this depth-oriented mask work with several hypotheses. First, I believed that masks used within in a ritual context can act as a bridge and facilitate the integration of unconscious material into conscious awareness. This is, indeed, what happened in my experiments with masks, as you will see in the coming chapters. Deeply buried unconscious material did arise through my work with masks. The ritual mask work not only brought unconscious material forward, it was instrumental in helping me integrate the material into conscious awareness, as I will explain throughout the rest of this book.

Second, I was interested in the idea that masks induce altered states of consciousness such as trances, which I had been encountering in both my research and my personal experiences with masks. The third area of interest stemmed from an intense curiosity about the mysterious other, the "spirit of the mask," which people have reported experiencing from ancient times through to the present day. My personal experience has been that I *do* enter into altered states of consciousness while wearing masks, and I *do* experience personalities that appear to be autonomous. The personalities certainly have seemed to be separate from my ego consciousness and, perhaps, separate from my psyche altogether, as I expound on in the final chapters of this book.

After years of study and research, I have not yet found the answers to the questions about the spirit of the mask. I am not sure the questions are even definitively answerable. What I have found is more questions in this regard. Although I am still in the midst of seeking the answers, and by no means consider myself to be an expert on this, I do my best to lay out my preliminary findings in the coming chapters.

Containing and Mirroring the Unconscious

I began with the idea that, at a minimum, masks function like other art forms such as painting and poetry, which are able to capture, contain, and mirror unconscious projections.[1] I found this to be true in my investigation with masks. By engaging my imaginal faculties, I was able to create external physical objects (the masks), based on inner experiences. Symbols poured forth from my unconscious - the Star, the Spark, the Void, the Horned One - and found expression in the masks. These unconscious symbols were projected onto the mask, which psychologically served as what Winnicott[2] referred to as a transitional object – an object that exists somewhere on the continuum between inner and outer experience.

I will attempt to explain in the coming chapters how, in wearing the masks within sacred rituals, I was able to re-absorb the unconscious material back into my body, my mind, and my emotional being after it had been made conscious by my work with the mask. I found that wearing the masks served to ground the ideas and notions contained in the arising symbols into physical, emotional, and even spiritual experiences. In this way, the symbols, which began as mental images, were transformed into emotional and physical experiences.

Through this work, I was able to isolate each symbol from the tangled mass of symbols vying for my attention. I was then able to consciously and deliberately work with each of the now more clearly defined symbols. As I began amplifying each symbol, I started to see where the material it signified had been enmeshed in my personality. I began to separate the psychic material represented by the symbol from the unconscious *prima materia*.

The importance of working with shadow material, particularly that which develops from psychological and emotional wounding, came forward during my work with the masks. Through this work I began to separate the cultural wound material from the personal wound material and was thereby able to start truly integrating them both.

Finally, my efforts continually circled back around to considering the connection between psychological initiation and masks, as well as the role masks play in integrating the patterns of creation and destruction, death and rebirth that surround rites of passage. As noted earlier, the archetype of initiation is often activated during times of distress when challenges emerge to thrust us forward into new ways of being in our inner and outer world.[3] Masks have historically been employed to help facilitate the oft-times mystifying process of initiation.[4] Although I was familiar with the relationship between masks and initiation, I had not expected my personal experience with masks to, essentially, follow a process comparable to initiation, as you will see in the following chapters.

The Spirit of the Mask

I began my investigation with the notion that the autonomous personality that arrives when a mask is donned represents a personal complex and the archetype that comprises the core of that complex. Complexes have been described as emotionally charged fragments of personality that contain personal material which centralizes around an archetypal core.[5] They are responsible for bringing shadow material up from the unconscious and expressing it out into the world. Archetypally-centered complexes are very powerful. They can be experienced as either positive or negative and often manifest as dissociative states we may be entirely unaware of at first.

After working extensively with the three masks, I am coming away with a newly formed hypothesis that further differentiates the layers of psyche approached through mask work. Based on my personal experiential exploration and my work with students, I now believe that masks have the potential to work on several different levels, depending on the psyche of the individual and how advanced they are in their self-knowledge and self-awareness, in other words, depending on how individuated the ego is.

Masking at Three Levels

Projections, Complexes and Archetypes

I propose that the first level approached in mask work has to do with projecting unconscious material onto the mask, so that it can be contemplated. In psychological terms, projection is described by Jung[6] as "the expulsion of a subjective content into an object...[and in the process] the subjective content becomes alienated from the subject and is, so to speak, embodied in the object."

The second level is working with personal complexes through masks. The third level is working with archetypes. Based on my experiences, I am starting to conjecture that there may be a fourth level of experience evoked by masks. This layer of work goes beyond the collective unconscious into a realm referred to as psychoidal, which I explain in the last chapter.

As mentioned above, I began with an idea that masks work like other art forms, acting as a container and mirror for personal projections. Although I cannot say for certain in the case of my students, it appears that when they first begin working with masks, they connect mostly with unconscious projections. As they go further into the work, they seem to move deeper into the shadow and begin dealing with complex-oriented material. This is as far as my students have seemed to go in their mask work during workshops and classes. Perhaps with more time and deeper engagement, they will begin to move into addressing deeper layers of psyche with their masks.

I believe that in the beginning of my work with masks, I was doing the same thing. Early on in working with masks, I could see that I was projecting items from the unconscious that were then being mirrored back to me. For example, the very first depth-oriented mask I created revealed a sense of inner division and multiplicity, which I was experiencing, but had not yet made fully conscious.

I then moved into working with my complexes through masks. With the Medusa mask, mentioned in Chapter One, I began working with complex-based material in a tangible way. My inner Victim Complex came forward into the mask and I was able to gain incredible insight into the insidious role the victim has played in my psyche.

With the three masks described in this book, I was working with projections and complexes, as you will see. Yet I believe that I moved beyond the personal shadow material and into deeper layers of the unconscious. The archetypal symbols that came forward in the Star, Void, and Horned One masks did not strictly address my personal projections and complexes. Although that was an important part of the process, it was not the only thing taking place.

The masks brought me deeper into psyche, plunging me into cultural complex material, such as the scapegoat (described in ch.15). The masks moved me to the third level, connecting me with powerful archetypal forces such as creation and destruction which exist in a deeper layer of psyche - the collective unconscious.

However, the most profound and mysterious experience occurred during the ritual with the Horned One mask (ch.17-19), which I believe moved me to an even deeper level of mask work that has to do with the *psychoidal* realm, which I define and explain in Chapter Twenty One.

With all of this background information in place, I now invite you behind the scenes in my mask workshop and in my own psyche as I introduce you to the masks and show them at work in my personal initiatory processes.

End Notes

1. McNiff, 2004
2. Winnicott, 1951
3. Henderson, 1967
4. Nunley & McCarty, 1998
5. Stein, 1998; Weinrib, 1991
6. Jung, as quoted in von Franz, 1972, p.12

9 MEETING THE GUIDE

You've been introduced to the tools involved in the creation of depth-oriented mask rituals. Now it's time to see the tools woven together and in action. In the following chapters I take you through three detailed examples of my work with three different masks. I explain each step in the process and share my discoveries with you, exactly as they occurred. You'll see how I used the tools to create each mask, make connections with archetypes and symbols, and then connect it to my psychological and emotional experience. You'll see examples of ritual, active imagination, art processes, and symbolic amplification and how I used them to (unknowingly at the time) activate a profound initiatory experience that has permanently altered me. As I share with you this intimate look at my work and my own psychic wounds, I ask you to hold this personal disclosure gently, treating it with the respect that all sacred therapeutic processes warrant. And I implore you to do the same with yourselves and your students.

It's important to note that during the time I was immersed in this depth oriented, art-based project, I had no idea where it would lead me. It turned out to facilitate a personal *coniunctio* experience. The alchemical *coniunctio* is the union of a pair of opposites which have first been separated from one giant mass, then separately purified, to then be reunited into a more clarified and refined whole. Though I had at the time been studying the cross-cultural connection between masks and initiation, I hadn't expected my work with masks to take me on an initiatory journey. It was only in retrospect, after the work was complete, that I realized the depths of what had actually occurred. Following this spark of curiosity has opened up new horizons of mystery and inquiry, as you'll see in the coming pages.

Let There Be Light

> *The stars shone forth as beacons proclaiming that each individual life was connected with the divine pattern, offering hope that the seemingly random events of daily life created a meaningful part in the universal scheme. Through his sympathy with the stars man, no longer a plaything of fate, became inspired with a feeling of destiny. It is as if the twinkling stars were little windows or eyes through which man glimpsed eternity.*
> ~Sally Nichols[1]

Dancing with Trickster

From the very beginning of my work with masks, the Trickster is usually the first archetype to come forward in my psyche and present itself as the subject for a mask. I have not been comfortable directly calling in the unpredictable energy of the Trickster and embodying it in a mask. From the beginning of the master's thesis project (from which this work is derived) I had been thinking about working with the Trickster archetype, but felt unsure of approaching it directly or inviting it in into my life in such a pronounced way. The very thought of doing this evoked a strong sense of fear, hesitation, and tentative feelings.

I talked with my wise council of thesis advisors about this, and it was suggested that I begin by opening myself to a less threatening archetype. I was reminded that the thesis process is difficult enough without bringing in shadow material that evokes immediate resistance. It was also noted that I may end up working with the Trickster anyway. Everyone agreed my dance with the Trickster tends to be some kind of central axis in my work. The Trickster appeared at the very beginning of my work with masks and has been showing up to stir the process throughout.

Mask One – First Encounters with the Guide

When I started exploring this depth-oriented mask work, I was unsure of how to approach the creation of the first mask. I felt as if I had entered into uncharted territory. Because, in fact, I had entered into unknown territory from the very beginnings of this foray. That is the nature of working with the unconscious. We are only partly conscious of what we are doing and why. There's something bigger, older and more powerful at play. Our egos can only grasp the tip of the iceberg. So, I began "in the dark" as it were, with a jumbled mass of my own *prima materia*. Then, piece by piece the process began to unfold until, eventually, I had a completed mask. Following is a snapshot of my process.

Identifying Archetypes and Symbols

The idea for the first mask came while engaging in activities that put me into the creative state, described earlier. It happened immediately after my thesis proposal meeting, when I first presented the scope of the work I was imagining. Sharing my ideas with respected mentors filled me with energy and excitement. I needed to release the intensity of energy that had built up over the course of the meeting, so I went for a hike at my favorite wilderness park.

Entering the Imaginal and Questing for a Vision

Before the hike, I set the intention that the experience would serve the function of a mini *Vision Quest*. This term is used to describe a Native American rite of passage which continues to be used for initiating a person from one phase of life into the next, such as adolescence to adulthood. In this type of ritual, the individual leaves the community and enters the natural world alone, without food or shelter. On a vision quest, one encounters literal objects and signs, such as plants, animals, and natural events. The external signs hold deeper symbolic meaning that can be used to interpret and reinterpret oneself and one's place in society. In this way, the natural world itself becomes the initiating force.[2]

I set off into the wilderness with the goal of evaluating the archetypes currently active in my psyche in hopes of receiving inspiration for my first mask. I held this intention as my primary focus. As I hiked I let my mind wander in a state of reverie while at the same time remaining consciously observant of the flow of thoughts, corresponding emotional states, physical sensations, and signs from nature. As I pondered the question of how to begin creating the first mask, I mentally reviewed all of the archetypes and symbols that have come up repetitively for me over the preceding two years. A few stood out more than others. They were more persistent in my psyche, showing up more often and over longer stretches of time.

Tracking the Movements of the Unconscious

Because I keep both art-based and written journals, it is fairly easy for me to track symbols and archetypes as they appear in my life over long periods of time. As mentioned earlier, the archetypes and symbols arrive in dreams, in active imaginations and waking reveries, in spontaneous art processes, and in synchronicities. I record them in written and visual form so that I can periodically review the symbolic messages from my unconscious and look for long-term patterns to emerge from the seemingly random and chaotic material. This helps me become more conscious of the symbolic messages coming from my unconscious, thus laying the groundwork for deeper explorations of the material that arises.

During the hike, many currently active archetypes came to me: The Trickster, the Magician, the Grandmother, the Wise Old Woman, the Crone, the Witch, the Healer, the Midwife, the Teacher, the Priestess, the Queen, the Storyteller, the Artist, and the Guide. As I hiked, I observed a white moth or butterfly continually crossing my path and flying in front of me, as if it were trying to guide me somewhere.

Noticing Synchronicities

Several months earlier, I wrote a fairy tale which had little white moths that served as guides to the heroine who had been spelled into a deep sleep, whereby she forgot her identity. The moths appeared and guided her to a place of remembrance. *Psyche* is the Greek word for butterfly. Butterflies and moths signify physical transformations as well as the metamorphoses of souls. The *ARAS Book of Symbols*[3] contains a lovely passage: "The butterfly is one of our most poetic images of psyche's self-renewal beyond even traumatic endings." The appearance of the white butterfly felt like an important signal, a synchronicity, which corresponded with the moment I began thinking about the Guide Archetype.

Through tacit knowing and intuition the guide became the principal archetype in my field of attention. I started thinking about the appearance, in spontaneous drawings and active imaginations, of what could possibly be my inner guide. The following drawing, which I'd created thirteen months earlier, is one of the items that immediately came to mind. From the moment I drew the masked face I had a sense that she, the masked one, is beckoning the viewer to follow her into the realm of the unknown. From the beginning, the image has evoked the notion that the masked figure represents a guiding force that leads one into and through the mysteries of transformation as represented by the ever-changing moon and death, a symbol of the ultimate transition.

Figure 6. Inner Alchemy Drawing

Calling in the Guide Archetype

In the weeks that followed the hike, I began to more seriously contemplate the notion of working with the Guide Archetype for my first mask. As I considered working with the guide, it began to make so much sense for me at that particular time in my life. First, I had recently reached a place in my personal depth work, and in my individual therapy, where I was becoming increasingly aware of the need to be gentle with myself. I was seeking a more delicate way to navigate my active, dynamic, and often intense psychic life. As I sat with the idea of working with the guide I began to realize that, not only was I yearning to call on the guide archetype to help me navigate the labyrinthine underworld of my psyche, but also that the Guide had already been presenting itself to my psyche. I simply had not been alert to it yet.

I began to sense that the process of creating my first thesis mask was growing from a combination of my emotional and psychological needs, mingled with the guide archetype itself showing up to guide the process, even before I was consciously aware of it. I realized there was an undeniable wisdom in consciously choosing an archetype that felt safe and approachable, rather than allowing any archetype that presented itself to be concretized into a mask.

Unfolding Symbols

As I circumambulated the idea of working with the guide, deeper layers of the symbol began to unfold for me. Of course, once I made the decision it seemed so obvious. I was seeking to become a guide for others, in terms of accessing the inner depths through expressive arts. I realized I was being guided to first get in touch with my inner guide in a truly conscious manner.

I also began to realize that, at the time, the guide part of me was in need of further development and integration. It was not a fully integrated, conscious part of my personality yet. But I knew that the Guide is actually a dominant feature of my latent personality. That had been showing up for years. People had many times asked me to be a guide to others in areas where I have extensive experience. Although I had previously taught art classes and co-lead psycho-spiritual and creative workshops, I had not yet consciously integrated my role as a guide. I hadn't fully stepped into it and claimed it as one of my stronger traits, despite ongoing encouragement to do so. I was frequently asked to teach workshops, yet I would often hesitate and sometimes even resist opportunities *without consciously knowing why.*

Connecting the Symbolic to Personal Process

After identifying the guide as the first archetype I wanted to work with, I began to recognize this as an area that was blocked, an area where perhaps there was some form of arrested development that had occurred. I had set the intention to create a process and a methodology that I could teach to others. I had not previously considered that I was fundamentally invoking the guide in embarking on this process.

Once I named the guide, I began to see it everywhere in my inner and outer life. As mentioned, it was showing up in my artwork, in my dreams and in active imagination for well over a year. I just hadn't made the conscious connection until this point.

Ritual – Invoking the Guide

Based on the connections I was starting to make with the Guide Archetype and my current stage of development, I intuitively knew it was time to begin working with the guide in a more embodied way. I knew I had to take it out of the realm of ideas and begin exploring it imaginally so that it could concretize into a clearer symbol I could turn into a mask. In other words, I knew it was time to experience the guide archetype on a deeper psychic level.

In order to proceed, I elected to do an Active Imagination. I set the intention to meet the Guide Archetype within and ask it for permission and guidance in creating a mask. I tape recorded the experience, which I do not normally do. I spoke everything that took place in my inner world and everything I experienced during the ritualized active imagination into a tape recorder in an attempt to be both participant and observer.

My goal was to stay consciously aware (even as I entered into altered states) and to track the experiences of my mind, body, emotions, and subtle energies. I also took care to note how I felt prior to ritual and how I felt during it. I also noted how I felt immediately afterwards, to see if any changes occurred on any level of my being.

Entering the Imaginal

I kept the structure of the ritual I formed around the active imagination basic. First, as noted above, I set the conscious intention to meet the guide within. Next, I created the appropriate psychic container for entering into an active imagination, as explained in Chapter Six. This includes: setting aside private, undisturbed time and space; departing from ordinary life and crossing an imaginal threshold into the non-ordinary realm; having the experience (and in this case, recording it); then coming back into ordinary awareness; and finally, reflecting on the experience.

In this case, the process consisted of: going into my bedroom where I could be alone and uninterrupted for at least an hour; lighting a candle and symbolically cleansing the space with incense; deep breathing and dropping into a meditative state, then bringing in percussive instruments to help further induce an altered state of consciousness; inviting the guide archetype to be present; and then entering into the active imagination.

The Guide Appears

Once the ritual container was set, I began the Active Imagination with a guided visualization that I have done before, which began with imagining myself standing before a great old willow tree. I imaginally entered the ancestor willow with the intention of moving down into its roots, to emerge into an underworld-type of experience, as I have done before.

Instead of being taken down into the underworld, as I had expected, my inner vision took me up the branches to a region of pure light. There, I met a guide who appeared to me as what I can best describe as a spark of divine light or a star-being. The experience was truly ineffable and words simply cannot accurately convey the experience but, for the sake of this document, I will do my best to explain it. The inner being I encounter revealed itself simultaneously as a being of light, a spark of light, as a celestial being, and as a star.

Qualities of the Guiding Star

I had an amazing and rather long imaginal journey in which the Guide Archetype showed me the essence of its being and the way it is able to move between any and all realms. It can cloak itself in what it described as "garments" in order to enter the material world. It is a spark of light that can transform itself into physical form. It represented this concept by showing me an image of a pearl of light being enclosed by many petals of a lotus which protect the spark within - hiding it at the very center of the lotus. The experience was very visual and quite stunning.

The guide then showed me that it can move in and out of matter at will. It is mercurial; changing to fit the environment. It is an androgynous shape-shifter that can take on any incarnation, any form, and any age. It is silvery and has a reflective, mirror-like surface that can reflect its surroundings. The mirroring capacity is the mechanism that allows it to move between and adapt to different realms. It demonstrated that it frequently takes on the appearance of the sky, and sometimes the mirror surface of water, which reflects the sky. It has a whole set of associated symbols that it showed me and I recorded into the voice recorder.

I came away from the experience with a very clear sense of the essential nature of this inner guide being and a clear visual of the mask I would soon create to represent, and presumably, embody it. I noted that before the ritual I felt a little anxious and nervous and that after the ritual I felt calm, peaceful, relaxed, restful, happy, and joyful, with a sense of genuine well-being. Following the journey experience (which started as an active imagination), I began to realize that the symbols of the spark of light and the star had been showing up in my dreams, art, and synchronicities for a very long time.

End Notes

1. Sally Nichols, 1980, p. 300
2. Foster & Little, 1992
3. Ronnberg & Martin, 2010, p. 234

10 A MASK IS BORN

Now that I had a clear picture of the archetype and symbol I would be working with, it was time to begin creating the mask. Following is a description of the steps I took to create the mask. Keep in mind that I am a trained artist, so my approach for this particular mask was more involved than need be. I have created many simple masks out of plaster strips and even papièr machè, personally and with students – to great results. The medium used to create the mask is less important than the symbolic work that follows. For more information and resources on constructing masks, visit my website: AlembicArts.com

Creating Mask One

Face Form

Before creating the guide mask, I decide to create a face form, which is a casting of my face on which to shape and mold the leather masks. (I had recently begun working with leather, finding that it lends itself nicely to performance masks, creating something akin to a "second skin"). This turned into its own noteworthy experience, which proved to be very alchemical. I spent a full day with my eldest son, making casts of my face and using various sculpting materials to create a face form…none of which worked out! Yet the day yielded interesting results in and of itself. A new body of non-wearable, nature-based masks emerged from this experiment, which I will explain briefly.

We began by casting my face in plaster strips, a process known as *life casting*. The experience was rife with death and rebirth symbolism. As the final strips were laid over my face, I became isolated and enclosed, like a caterpillar in a cocoon. Although I have experienced plaster face casting before, this time it was uncomfortable, psychologically and emotionally, to be cut off from my environment. I felt helpless. The world could still see me, but I could not see it. I felt vulnerable. I had to concentrate in order to relax.

When the cast was finally pulled off, the experience was like a rebirth, a reemergence back into the world. I will not go into detail of the rest of the process, but suffice it to say that I felt like an alchemist in her workshop: mixing substances and observing their reactions; watching things liquefy, then solidify, heat up, and dry out.

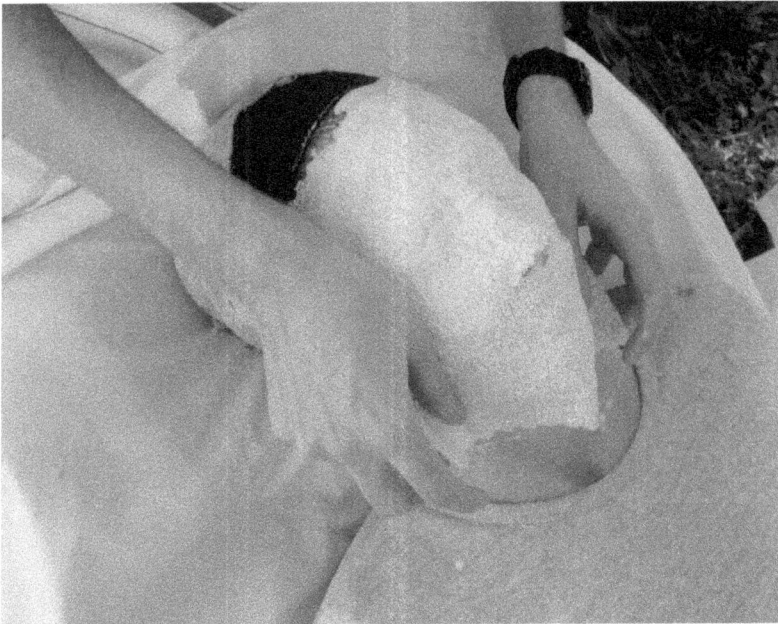

Figure 7. Face Cast

It is also important to note the presence of the Trickster archetype which churned my neatly planned project into a series of false starts and side-tracks which yielded unexpected yet interesting results. I attempted, and failed, to make a face form four times over several days. Every time I thought I had it figured out, the process would change and go awry. Once my frustration subsided, I saw that each attempt was a work of art unto itself, even though I was still without a face form.

Finally, my fifth attempt yielded a viable face form, pictured below. In this image, I finally decided to bring into existence the black and white face I had been seeing in my mind's eye. The face form felt like a safe format in which to contain the image of the Tricksterish polarities represented by black and white. I was not ready to wear the mask of the Trickster, but I could pay homage to it and honor its presence by making it the face upon which all of my leather masks are formed.

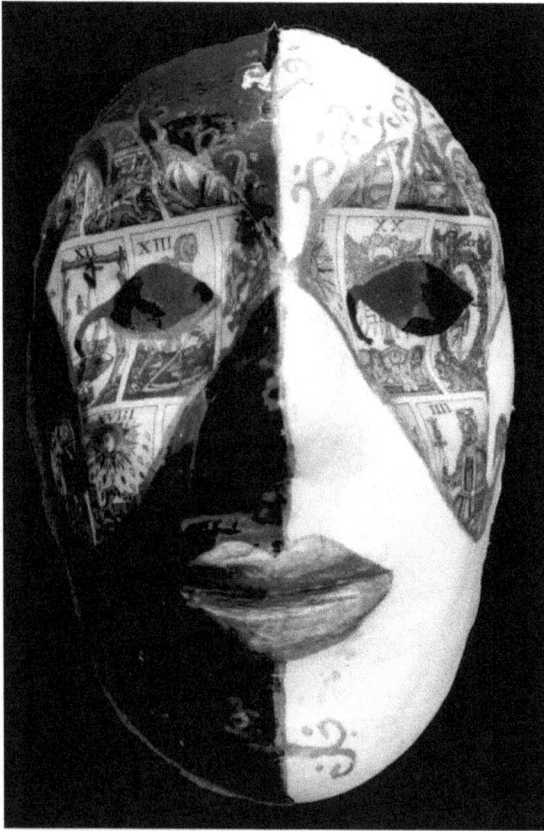

Figure 8. Face Form

Making the (Guiding) Light Mask

After I finally created a workable face form, I began creating the mask as it appeared to me in the imaginal journey. I created the mask out of leather, an explanation of which is beyond the scope of this book. As I formed, shaped, painted and adorned the mask, I engaged in art-based methods such as dialoguing with the materials and doing active imagination with the mask as an art object, which I had not, at this point, placed on my face.

While I had seen a basic picture of it in my mind during the first active imagination, the details were not fully formed. So, I interacted with the mask as an intelligent "other" and asked it to guide me in its own creation. I would ask it questions like: what color(s) are you? Where do you want the mirrors place? What else do you want to be decorated with? And so forth…

While creating the mask and imaginally working with the materials, the mask indicated that it was being created for performance purposes. It implied it is to be worn before an audience; it is to be witnessed. It hinted at having a myth and a performance as part of its life cycle, similar to the Medusa mask I described in Chapter One. What came up during the imaginal work was that a part of my personal integration process, a step in my transformation cycle, was to recover the inner storyteller and performance artist hiding in the shadows, awaiting more full expression.

These dialogues with the mask triggered deep wounds and stirred shadow material locked away in my psyche. I noticed myself feeling inexplicable fear, insecurity, and anxiety as I dialogued with the mask. I felt an unsettling discomfort just thinking about being on a stage and being the center of attention. As I began working with the shadow material that was stirring, I dropped into a deep-seated fear of being seen and heard based in my childhood. As a child, I frequently felt safest in my environment when I was invisible. Being seen had sometimes led to unwanted attention which ended in traumatic experiences. Although I had already processed through this issue on a psychological and emotional level, the fear was still lodged in my body and no amount of reasoning had been able to shift the felt experience of this fear.

Suddenly, the idea occurred to me that, perhaps, I was undergoing an initiation, an alchemical transformation in my own psyche through this mask work and that the return and re-aggregation into my community, the sharing of the boon, would be teaching others and eventually, performing with the masks. With this realization, I felt an acute sense of panic. My stomach tightened. I felt short of breath and a knot formed in the back of my throat. I realized I was touching into important unconscious material that I was finally ready to integrate and shift on a fundamental, corporeal level.

After the general shape of the mask was in place, but while I was still early in the creation process, I got a strong intuitive hunch that I needed to begin working with it in ritual, even though it was not yet complete. At this time I also started having repeated spontaneous visions of a black mask, which I will expand upon in later chapters. Below is a photograph of me wearing the completed Guiding Light/Star mask.

Figure 9. Spark of (Guiding) Light Mask/ Star Mask

Ritual – Working with The Guiding Star Mask

I set the ritual container in a similar manner as described above and in Chapter Seven. Again, I describe into my digital recorder what I am seeing and feeling. When the ritual stage was set, I called in the spirit of the guide mask and invited it to come forward and communicate with me. I put the mask on, breathed deeply and dropped in, as explained in Chapter Seven. I waited until I felt a shift in my awareness and a shift in my body, which is difficult to articulate, yet somatically palpable. I felt the presence of another being, the Guide. My body began to spontaneously move in steady rhythm; my weight shifting back and forth between each foot. Words popped into my mind: "balance, balancing, mercurial being walking the line of balance…on the globe…balancing on the sphere…"

I felt my awareness being pulled up out of my body. In my inner vision I was again taken upward. This time, I was pushed out into the universe. I was looking at many galaxies, then our galaxy, then our solar system, and then finally the planet Earth. I saw Earth from the perspective of a star out in space. It frightened me. I felt shaken. The experience was hard for me to hold, to stay with.

The Earth seemed so fragile and vulnerable from the perspective of a star. I felt lonely and isolated out in space. I felt like my life was small, insignificant, a blip on the cosmic radar. I felt as if my whole existence was tenuous and irrelevant to the larger forces of the material universe. I did not like the feeling. I was reminded of a series of dreams I had been having, over the previous couple of years, about objects in space hovering above; sometimes crashing down or colliding with the Earth. Then my mind raced backward in time, through years of deep-space related dreams that stretch back into my childhood.

I felt the presence of the star being I encountered in the first ritual. I saw the brilliant spark of light in my mind's eye and it began to speak to me. The star-like guide talked about movement, the constant dynamic movement of the universe and everything in it. It said that the idea of standing still is an illusion. It talked about the law of balance. Then it said things about my consciousness being up above and down below simultaneously. It said that I am in both places, above and below. It told me it is the spirit in matter, consciousness in material form, and that it is part of the One, the All That Is. It explained that it exists outside of the laws of the universe, that it is ambiguous and holds the paradox of being the pieces and the whole. It said it stands at the center of this mystery, holding it all together.

The spirit of the mask declared: "In my mirror you will see many things - things that may frighten you, things that may delight you. I will help you. I will guide you to be able to hold what is in the mirror, to be able to look into the mirror and see the reality that is reflected there. I will help you do this." For a full transcript of the dialogue between myself and the spirit of the mask see Appendix A.

Throughout the entire experience, I was aware of the presence of the guide, the "other" moving and speaking through me, and I was also aware of myself, the Tina-ego-personality I am familiar with. The two were coexisting in these precise moments through the vehicle of the mask. It was a very profound experience for my psyche – physically, mentally, and emotionally. I did my best to note into the recorder the details of my encounter with the mask, including the somatic and emotional experiences that occurred during the ritual, although much of it was difficult to adequately capture in words. The complete description of this experience can be found in Appendix A.

Shining a Light on a Mystery

The Guide Archetype appeared to me in the form of a being that was simultaneously symbolized by the star and the divine spark of light. I began the project with the notion of meeting my inner guide. My understanding, derived from communicating with the mask "spirit", is that the Guide Archetype has many forms. One of its forms is as a star, the Guiding Star.

The Star is comprised of light. The same light that inhabits a celestial star is mirrored in a diminutive form as a spark of light, which is, essentially, a scaled down speck of starlight that animates the material realm. The star and the spark are of the same essence. The difference is that one exists in large scale above in the heavens, and one is scattered below on the earth. The spark is to the star as the drop of rain is to the ocean. Elementally rain and ocean are the same thing – water. Likewise, the spark and the star are quintessentially light.

The symbol of the light, represented macrocosmically as a star and microcosmically as an inner spark, came forward and made itself known in a more concrete and embodied way through the work with the mask. The symbol of the guide as a divine light, as a guiding inner and outer star, began to open to me in incredible ways – intellectually and emotionally - once I had a felt experience of the subtle energy of it and had the vibration of it in my body.

After the ritual encounter, the symbols of the star and the spark of light became containers around which myriad associations began collecting. I began sleeping eating, thinking, breathing the image of the light within (spark) and without (star). Then, a whole new network of associations occurred and a new web of information began to form, which will be explained more in the coming chapters.

I had to take time to sit with and digest the material that came through. It took time for a cohesive picture to unfold. I had to be patient and persistent in order for the themes and patterns of the unconscious material the mask was indicating to begin coming together on a conscious level.

Guided Forward

This second ritual pointed to the next step, which is amplifying the archetypes that had arisen thus far: the guide, the star, and the spark of light. How did I do this? I looked at where the archetypal symbols had appeared, first in my own life, and then examined their occurrences in the history, art, and literature of various cultures. The next chapter details what I learned through archetypal amplification.

11 ILLUMINATING SYMBOLS

Amplifying the Archetypes and Symbols

As explained in Chapter Seven, *archetypal amplification* is simply the process of conducting research on how and where a symbol or archetype has appeared throughout history and cultures. It helps to gather information through as many avenues as possible – myths, fairy and folk tales, images, dictionary and encyclopedic definitions, previous research on, or studies of the phenomenon, etc.

Once a more global picture of the archetype has formed, it's important to see what aspects of the archetypal stories and images feel most personally relevant. It's also important to keep in mind the larger scope of qualities and characteristics of the archetype, knowing that sometimes the things that we're initially unconscious of, or even resistant to, can end up holding the most relevant and important insights.

Following is what I discovered through amplifying the Guide, the Star and the Spark of Light.

The Guide

For me, the Guide Archetype functioned in a manner similar to that of a gatekeeper, a threshold guardian that acted as an entry point into the deeper psychic symbols that followed. Through the process of amplification I learned that the Guide Archetype, related to the Roman messenger god Mercury, acts as a divine *psychopomp*, moving between realms and crossing boundaries.[1] The word psychopomp derives from the Greek word psychopompos, meaning conductor of souls, which combines the root words *psyche*, meaning breath, spirit, and soul, with *pompos,* meaning conductor or guide.[2]

Psychopomps in Greek mystery rites lead the initiate to the descent into the depths and then guides them through the underworld.[3] This can be likened to a descent into the realm of imagination, into the underworld of psyche, the shadow lands of the unconscious mind. Psychopomps, or spirit guides, typically appear as adept border crossers and as ones who walk between the worlds.

They are Tricksters who will do whatever it takes to reach their destination and who are shape-shifters who can change their appearance to adapt to various times and places.[4] They are often represented as magical figures able to facilitate healings in unforeseen ways and guide others through deep transformations such as death. In depth psychology, the psychopomp is a mediator between the world of the conscious mind and the unconscious realms.[5]

The connections between the guide and the Trickster, in terms of shape shifting and boundary crossing, both surprised and intrigued me. The guide is said to know the architecture of the other realm, rather than being the intelligent force behind its creation. The guide often appears as a teacher and healer. The guide can be likened to the spirit guides of the shamans who assist them as they journey beyond this world, into supernatural realms.[6] It is an archetype that frequently appears in conjunction with initiation and changes in state or life circumstance.

Hermes, the Greek version of Mercury, is an important threshold deity. The Archive for Research in Archetypal Symbolism[7] contains a passage that illuminates the multi-functional nature of Hermes the divine guide: "The presence of Hermes is significant. As psychopompos, he not only guided the souls of the dead to the Underworld, but also those living heroes whose fate required that they make the dangerous initiation journey." After conducting research on the guide, I was amazed and thrilled that my personal guide seems to have taken on archetypal qualities of the guide as it appears in myth, literature, and depth psychology. The guide that appeared to me was a shape-shifter, boundary crosser, it spoke of ambiguity and paradox – all archetypal qualities of the Guide.

The Star

The Star revealed itself as a primary aspect of the guide for me personally. As I began examining my environment, I realized that the star has appeared frequently in my art journals and in my life prior to the imaginal journey where I was formally introduced to the Guiding Star Archetype. It was, actually, a friend who first pointed out the prevalence of the star as a symbol in my life. I have often been gifted with objects shaped as or imprinted with stars; I have jewelry and clothes with stars. Stars appear often in my art and as objects placed around my home. My friend was able to walk into my life and see a symbol all around me, which I was so surrounded by and accustomed to seeing that I never consciously took note of it.

Furthermore, nearly every time I have pulled a tarot card from one of my decks or decks belonging to friends in the two years prior to creating this mask, it has been the Star card. An even stranger synchronicity that occurs, that I had been recording but not fully connecting, is that I find star shapes out in the world in the form of all kinds of random objects: a star -shaped lens popped out of a pair of children's sunglasses; a baby bootie on the beach covered in blue stars, little plastic stars, several glass stars, star sequins, star confetti, a star earing - all in the preceding year! I keep all of the objects that I find in random places, mostly on the ground, and I now have a substantial collection of star-shaped found objects.

The star is a universal symbol, appearing in all cultures and times and therefore, it can accurately be considered an archetype. The ARAS Book of Symbols sums up the power of the star as a symbol: "There are no peoples in the world who have not projected onto the starry heavens the preeminent forces and myths of their cosmos."[8] After the star/spark revealed itself to me during my inner imaginal journey, and offered itself up as a mask, I began to research the historical and cross-cultural occurrence of the star symbol, as well as Jungian interpretations of its significance.

Historical Perspectives of the Star Archetype

In ancient times, the province of the stars was regarded as the domain of divine, eternal beings. Consequently, folklore traditions around the world say that when you see a shooting star, you are witnessing the moment a soul comes to earth and a child is born. When a new star appeared in the heavens it was a sign that somewhere on Earth a great personality was born who would change the fate of humankind.[9] It was the star of Bethlehem which alerted the three magi to the birth of the Christ child, the birth of god into human form. In ancient China and in the Roman Empire, when an extraordinary person died, the astrologers searched the sky for a new star because they believed that at death the soul would return to the firmament to once again become a star.[10] Through tales such as these, the star has been associated with the great transitional mysteries of birth and death.

Furthermore, in ancient Egypt, the part of the psyche that is immortal and oriented toward the spirit realm was represented by the *Ba,* or soul, which was often depicted as a star. It symbolized the part of the person which transcended death, accompanying the Sun God through the sky as a never-setting star.[11] The Egyptian sky goddess Nut was depicted as giving birth to the stars through her great celestial body, similar to the way the unconscious births consciousness from its depths. For thousands of years stars have served as a primary navigational tool, orienting the traveler, just as the light of consciousness helps us navigate the darkness of the unconscious by orienting us to images and symbols offered up from the depths of the psyche.[12]

For alchemists the star symbolized the human imagination with its ability to shed light on, transform, and ultimately, to transcend the laws of matter. The famous alchemist Paracelcus thought of the star as the "light of nature", the intrinsic and distinctive individual spirit that resides in the center of each person.[13] The star also represents the human mysteries of sleeping and dreaming and the great mysteries of nature: death, and regeneration.[14] Stars evoke a sense of infinity and eternity in the earthbound gazer. They signify the eternal essence and unique, individualized nature of the personality.[15] This is the content that has been projected onto the star.

Psychological Perspectives of the Star Archetype

Psychologically speaking, Jung[16], attributes the symbol of the star to the archetype of the Self, the symbol of the individual and unique aspects of each person. From a depth psychological standpoint, the symbol of the star points to the process of individuation as the unifying of disparate parts of a personality into a synchronized whole. Foremost Jungian analyst Marie Louise[17] von Franz connects the star, the guide, and individuation succinctly in the following quote: "...the guiding star is the principle of individuation. It's that which guides one toward the absolute individual meaning of one's own individual life, one's innermost divine or cosmic destiny." According to von Franz, Jung taught that the star symbolizes that part of the personality that survives death; the spiritual part of the psyche.[18]

As stated by von Franz[19], the star or spark of light correlates to eternity, divinity, immortality, destiny, and individuality. She illustrates the psychic implications of the star archetype by analyzing an ancient dream from Sumerian history. Her interpretation of the dream has been pivotal to my personal understanding of what the symbol of the star means to me at this time in my life, so I include an examination of it below.

Gilgamesh and His Star

The 4600 year old dream of Gilgamesh (from the Mesopotamian Gilgamesh epic) is one of the oldest recorded dreams in history. The dream, recounted in the myth, is attributed to Gilgamesh, believed to be a real king unto whom mythic events were later overlaid.[20] It is unclear if the dream recounted was an actual dream of the living man, or simply a part of the myth. In the dream, a star falls from the heavens and lands on Gilgamesh. According to von Franz,[21] his star represents his unique destiny falling upon him. The star is too heavy for him to lift. Laden down with his star, he is surrounded by people who gather around and kiss his star's feet. Von Franz interprets the star as signifying Gilgamesh's uniqueness, his individual, immortal soul. Her analysis of this ancient dream is instructive and holds important information for my own psyche. Since reading this, many years ago, this dream and her interpretation have stayed with me and repeatedly replay in my mind. My psyche continues to circumambulate this reading of the star. Here it is in von Franz's own words.[22]

> That [when his star lands on him] is the moment his unique destiny befalls him, literally falls on his back. That means that just as Christ had to carry his cross, Gilgamesh now has to carry the burden of having to become the unique, chosen individual he was meant to be, a task which he has avoided by being an ambitious, collective man. Until the star fell upon him, Gilgamesh thought he was a great man. He was a king, he was a hero....But now he has to see that that is not much. What the people worship is that star stone, that greater thing in him and not his collective power....They prostrate themselves before the star, which is his true greatness.
>
> [The star falling upon Gilgamesh indicates that] he has now to follow his unique destiny instead of fulfilling a collective role. And this proves to be no glorious call, but a heavy burden to him. There is a teaching in the dream: don't take all the honor and compliments the people give you for yourself. It is the star upon you they worship. It's your necessity to become a unique individual. That's what they worship in you - not you. And that is your heaviest load...Because following your star means isolation, not knowing where to go, having to find out a completely new way for yourself instead of just going on the trodden path everybody else runs along. That is why there's been a tendency in humans to project the uniqueness and greatness of their own inner self onto outer personalities.

Projection of the Star

Von Franz[23] goes on to say that it is much easier to become a student, servant, admirer, or imitator of a great personality, than it is to follow your own star. Few people follow their own star because it is a task that proves to be a heavy burden. Following your star, the unique expression of your personality, often leads to isolation, to not knowing how to proceed, to having to carve out a completely new path rather than plodding along the same path your peers travel along. She says that as an alternative to this, most people place the preeminent qualities of their deep inner self onto outer figures. Those who display outstanding qualities often attract the projections of the star, which creates the temptation to become identified with the projections and thereby become inflated. This leads to a distorted and unrealistic opinion of oneself, the proverbial puffed up ego.

For the person doing the projecting, there can be either a positive or negative result. Projection is neither good nor bad; the effect ultimately depends on what one does with it. On the positive side, the admiration one feels toward the person holding the projection can bring about significant learning. If the person projected upon is truly great, like Mother Theresa for example, a person can be inspired to develop their own inner wisdom which leads to great acts. Conversely, and von Franz says more frequently, projecting one's star leads to an infantile belief that the greater personality can do all the work for you and that you can simply bask in the great teacher's glory. This leads to a loss of a solid sense of self and of one's own unique purpose. The danger, as von Franz[24] states it is that: "The star, the uniqueness of the personality, is projected and one is fascinated by the person out there instead of following one's inner authority."

The conscious and psychologically-oriented way to utilize the mechanism of projection in healing psyche is summarized nicely in Jung's analysis of the star symbol appearing in a woman's dream, as is recounted in the Vision Lectures Series.[25] In the Vision Lectures, Jung talks about the appearance of the star in one of his patient's dreams. In the dream she takes the star out of her body, projecting it outward into an external form. Of this Jung[26] says:

> Yes she objectifies that idea or intuition of the Self [symbolized by a star] in a visible form and makes an idol of it. That seems to us almost heathenish, for we labor under the impression that we could not make images of sacred things, of the idea of god, for

instance, because it would be idolatry. Apparently her unconscious in in favor of it, however…it must first be objectified, concretized, and then follows *betrachten,* contemplation.

She puts the star, signifying the Self archetype, outside of herself in order to dis-identify with it. Jung articulates that as long as you carry the symbol within, you are identical to it; you think "this is inside me, I am this." There is danger that the ego will become identified with the archetypal symbol. Jung says that first comes identification which then automatically triggers an inflation. Jung[27] illustrates psychological inflation in the following:

> You see, an ordinary human being who identifies with the creator thinks as if he were the creator, but if he succeeds in objectifying the creator as different from himself, then he himself, the gas bag, collapses; then he returns to human proportions and realizes he is not the creator.

Enlivening a Symbol

Jung describes the enlivening of a symbol or object. We objectify it by creating it as an image that exists outside of our selves, in my situation, the mask. Once we have created an external representation of the symbol, in this case the star, we can project unconscious content onto the image or object, filling it with energy and life. Once the image is externalized, and not until then, it can be worked with, or as Jung says, contemplated. By creating a representation of the celestial light being I encountered, in the form a star, I was able to form a relationship to the symbol as well as the psychic material it signifies.

According to Jung, through contemplation or "adoration" of the object representing the divine, both the object and the divine being it represents are filled with energy. It is an ancient and, Jung says, primitive idea that offerings give strength to the god, the archetype.[28] I find it interesting to consider that, according to this notion, the star as a consummate symbol of the divine is somehow enlivened by my work with it as a mask. Not only am I enriched, but the symbol itself is enriched as well.

The Spark of Light

Throughout literature and religion the spark is represented as an animating essence, a fertile principle that bursts forth igniting creation or destruction. The ARAS Book of Symbols contains an apt description of the spark's power and essence.[29] "Thus the spark embodies the incendiary potential of ideas, which can plant the seed for a new invention, scientific discovery or artistic creation, as well as spark a revolution powerful enough to reconfigure the entire world order." Ancient Greek philosophers believed that the human soul was made of star-stuff distributed as sparks of light that animate each and every living body. The Gnostics also conceived of the soul as being a spark of light, descended from heaven and trapped in the darkness of matter, awaiting its return the realm of heavenly light.[30]

In alchemy the scintilla were considered tiny sparks of light scattered across the earth and finely mingled with matter. The alchemists believed that, upon contemplation, the sparks shone in the darkness of matter, revealing themselves to the adept. When gathered together these sparks, the scintilla, formed the alchemical gold. For Jung, this gathering process corresponded with individuation. The scintilla correspond with the multiple centers of personality that exist within a single individual, a phenomenon he repeatedly observed in his clinical practice. Jung found that when a person becomes conscious of the multiple centers of personality within, they can begin extracting them from complexes and gather them together into a more integrated whole, the Self, the alchemical gold.[31]

Jung draws a direct parallel between the star and the spark of light, ascribing both symbols to the archetype of the Self, the individualized aspects of each person. In Jung's words, the Self is the "[G]erm of the supreme principle...in [its] most individual form; the individual light spark."[32]

Dionysus as Spark

In both Greek mythology and in depth psychology, the Dionysian principle is said to be the individual spark of creation that dwells within the human soul.[33] The Dionysian creation myth is filled with remarkable difficulty. Illegitimate son of Zeus and Semele, Dionysus falls victim to the vengeance of the dark aspect of Zeus' wife, Queen Hera, while still in his mother's womb. Hera tricks Semele, persuading her to confront Zeus in his true form. The sight of a god in his full power is too much for Semele, who dies six or seven months pregnant. Zeus sews the infant Dionysus into his thigh, where he spends his final months, gestating in the father. It is not long before jealous Hera has the infant Dionysus torn to bits by the Titans– in other words, he was dismembered.[34]

The Titans devour the pieces of Dionysus, swallowing him up and consuming his flesh. Edinger[35] says: "In punishment for the Titans' dismemberment of Dionysus, Zeus had hurled a thunderbolt at them, which had reduced them to dust, but that dust had little sparks of Dionysus scattered in it because they had all eaten him." The Titan dust eventually came to be used in the creation of humans and it is said that all humans are made out of Titan dust containing the Dionysian spark. According to this myth, we all, therefore, carry the Dionysian spark within.[36]

Dionysus represents the creative spark. Edinger[37] says that creativity is a particularly important aspect of Dionysus, from a psychological standpoint. His creativity is not methodical, as it is for the god Hephaestus, the master craftsman. Dionysian creativity is the inspired, almost intoxicating creativity in which the unconscious springs up and bursts out in an ecstatic frenzy.[38] The following quote from Jung[39] nicely illustrates the nature of Dionysian creativity and the way it can possess a person:

> [The creative forces] have you on the string and you dance to their whistling, to their melody. But inasmuch as you say that these creative forces are in…me or anywhere else, you cause an inflation, because man does not possess creative powers, he is possessed by them.

As stated previously, recognizing that the spark of creative inspiration comes from a source beyond us helps prevent us from inflation.

In Crete, Dionysus was known as the "god of the light that ripens."[40] Kerenyi[41] explains that the star Sirius was associated with

Dionysus in his form noted by Pindar as the "pure light of high summer" which ripened the vineyards over which Dionysus, as god of wine, presides. The rise of the star Sirius marked the beginning of the year in Egypt and the annual swelling of the Nile which brought both death and fertile new life in its wake. Sirius was considered an ambivalent star, signaling both destruction and creation, further connecting it to the ambivalent Dionysus who was considered to be the god of creative inspiration and destructive instincts. He was said to evoke both ecstasy and terror, much like the dog-star Sirius.[42]

Dionysus brings change, and so is, in part, a Trickster. Dionysus is a traveler and a wanderer. He is neither householder nor father. He and his rites are found in the wild places, outside the bounds of the civilized world.[43] Dionysian energy upsets the power principle as it presents itself in the stiff authority figure of his opposite, the Senex. He lives outside of the laws. He is a border dweller and boundary crosser, and not surprisingly, he is also known as the god of the mask,[44] Edinger[45] says of Dionysus:

> [H]e would appear unexpectedly in a new place, bringing excitement, joy, and terror, and changing what was there before…What Dionysus brings is wild, spontaneous, inspired behavior…There is ecstasy on the one hand and terror on the other, and the whole potential for inner transformation.

This research marked the beginnings of being introduced to the Dionysian principle behind mask work and within in my own psyche. At this point in my process, I still had no idea where I was being led. As the mystery unfolded over the coming years, I came to see that Dionysus resides at the center of this work, an apt place for the Trickster-like Greek god of the mask.

End Notes

1. Larsen, 1990
2. Liddell & Scott, nd
3. Kerenyi, 1986; Hillman, 1979
4. Hyde, 1998
5. Kerenyi, 1986; Hillman, 1979
6. Hillman, 1979
7. ARAS Record 3Ja.174
8. Ronnberg & Martin, 2010, p.18
9. von Franz & Boa, 1987
10. von Franz & Boa, 1987
11. von Franz & Boa, 1987
12. Ronnberg & Martin, 2010
13. Jung, 1967
14. Ronnberg & Martin, 2010
15. Jung, 1930; Nichols, 1980; von Franz & Boa, 1987
16. Jung, 1930-34
17. von Franz & Boa, 1987, p. 283
18. von Franz & Boa, 1987
19. von Franz & Boa, 1987
20. Wilkinson, 2010
21. von Franz & Boa, 1987
22. von Franz & Boa, 1987, p. 70-71
23. von Franz & Boa, 1987
24. von Franz & Boa, 1987, p. 74
25. Jung, 1930-34
26. Jung, 1930-34, p. 1160
27. Jung, 1930-34, p. 1161
28. Jung, 1930-34
29. Ronnberg & Martin, p. 86, 2010
30. Hoeller, 2002; Layton, 1987; Mead, 1921
31. Edinger, 1995
32. Jung, 1930-34, p. 1159
33. Edinger, 1994
34. Edinger, 1994; Fierz-David, 1980; Kerenyi, 1976; Otto, 1965
35. Edinger, 1994, p. 145
36. Edinger, 1994
37. Edinger, 1994
38. Edinger, 1994; Kerenyi, 1976; Otto, 1965; Deutsch, 1969
39. Jung as cited in Edinger, 1994, p. 148

40. Kerenyi, 1976, p. 279
41. Kerenyi, 1976
42. Kerenyi, 1976
43. Edinger, 1994, p. 143
44. Kerenyi, 1976
45. Edinger, 1994, p. 143-144

12 DECODING MESSAGES

Before I get into interpreting and applying the symbolic messages to my personal process, let's quickly review the steps I took in creating and working with the Guiding Light mask. The first step was identifying an archetype or symbol I wished to work with. As mentioned, I have also begun with creating a mask first and then working with it to see what archetypes or symbols it contains and reflects. Both approaches work well - and which one is used, depends on the starting point. For this one, I started by choosing the archetype - or so it seemed at the time. (I later began to realize that it may have actually chosen me).

For this mask, I began by isolating the Guide Archetype from the myriad archetypes that had been showing up. Next, I created a simple ritual and did an active imagination to meet my inner guide. That step yielded a clearer picture of the guide archetype, as it lives in me, revealed as a star and spark of light. From the active imagination, I came away with an idea, inspiration and general image of what the mask was going to look like.

From there I began creating the mask using art therapy processes such as dialoguing with the image and interpreting it. While I was still in the process of creating it, I began working with it in a ritual setting. This was done by creating ritual conditions, as already explained, donning the mask and "dropping in." This gave me an even more refined understanding of the archetypes and symbols I was working with in this mask. I then amplified the archetypes and symbols to see how others have understood them. I particularly focused on the musings of depth psychologists, as this is the focal point of my work with psyche. Finally, I reflected on all that I had experienced and learned in order to better understand how it applies to my psychological healing and development. This final step is crucial to integrating this type of depth oriented mask work.

Mining for the Gems

Why was this work so instructive for me? What did I learn and where did it lead me? As I reflected on what had occurred, I found that the idea of the Self archetype represented as a star is quite powerful for me. Through this work I began to identify my personal experience of continually approaching the Self archetype in my creative and depth psychological work. The most important idea that has come forward thus far is the danger of becoming identified with the Self and with the projections of the star, and the subsequent danger of inflation. As I reflect, I begin to see the ways this has come up for me, particularly in my role as an artist and a poet.

I have long espoused a belief that there is a creative energy that moves through me, that it is greater than me and that I am not the source of. On a conscious level, this is what I have always believed, and still believe. However, the fact that this is the symbol that has shown up and asserted itself in my psyche has caused me to pause and reflect more deeply on these notions.

I asked myself:

What is the converse of this conscious belief?

What are the ideas I consciously rejected and relegated to the shadow in order to develop the conscious attitude that I am a mere channel of creative forces far greater than me?

I began to wonder…

Is the appearance of this symbol telling me that not all of me believes this and that there is a part of me that either is, or is in danger of becoming, identified with the Self and subsequently, of becoming inflated? Do I carry anyone else's projections onto my "star" – that part that is "not me," but something greater? At the time of this writing, the jury is still out.

Next, I began examining the ways I have been dodging and avoiding my own unique destiny – both the dark and the light of it. I started to see how I have been pushing away, dissociating from and denying parts of my life experiences that have been difficult and unsavory. My work with the mask helped open up the idea that I have been, in part, projecting my star out onto others instead of living it for myself. I began to see that although it is not the entire story, there have been ways and places in which I have done this.

There have been places where I have stayed small, I stayed invisible, I hid. Through working with the mask I came to examine the fact that I am sometimes uncomfortable with attention, still. There is a part of me that is timid when it comes to sharing my creative work, especially performing before an audience. At the same time, there is a part of me that is attracted to it. There is a part of me to which it feels natural, innate, intrinsic. To others my inner artist, expresser and performer is obvious. People project a confidence onto me that I do not always personally experience.

Making the Unconscious Conscious

Through working with the Guiding Light mask, I have started to examine previously unconscious patterns of keeping myself incredibly busy accomplishing and achieving in the external world. As I grew older I became focused on being the best mom I could be, being the most dependable employee, an over-achieving student, etc. (Like Gilgamesh being a successful "man of the world"). In striving to be responsible, I have sometimes neglected my innate gifts and latent talents. In doing this I, in essence, abandon my own metaphorical inner star.

This is an area of my life that has been difficult to reconcile in my adult years. I feel a push-pull dynamic between the responsible provider and the artist that seeks to create with wild abandon. These two sides of me have been locked in a battle since I became a mother and provider many years ago. This is an area where the split between a conscious sense of duty and deep unconscious creative stirrings is particularly pronounced.

Through the mask I started to come into relationship with disparate parts that have been previously difficult to integrate. I began realizing that bouncing between allowing and denying spontaneous creative impulses is one of my core issues. It is an issue that can at times block me from living fully into my creative potential, into my uniqueness and individuality. For example, the parts of my personality that are adept at guiding, teaching, presenting and performing to an audience are strong yet were relatively undeveloped at the time I was doing this work.

Working with this mask helped me step into a larger role as a teacher and guide in the realms of creative depth work. I also became increasingly aware of the ways in which the creative impulses that move freely through me often do not find their way to full expression, and when they do, they are often not gifted to a larger audience or shared with my community.

Integrating the Wild and the Civilized

Through the work with the mask, I came into contact with a side of me that is adventurous and uninhibited in expression – a side that I have frequently repressed in order to maintain a busy and demanding schedule. I have always known that I have an untamed, uncivilized one inside me. I indulged this part of myself for years but began repressing her in order to adapt to the demands of supporting and raising my sons. I was ready to integrate this part of me more fully into my daily reality.

Through my work with the Guiding Light mask I touched into a deep desire to integrate the wild and creative and the civilized and responsible aspects of my personality and to hold the tension of these opposite ways of being to find the a new, third way. I have experienced the two extremes of wild abandon and poised civility and have found that my soul does not thrive fully, cannot be fully expressed, at either end of the spectrum. I must find my unique spot somewhere in the middle of these two poles.

The work the mask is pointing to is also about holding the opposites of my instinctual inner nature and the outer civilized world in a way that is creative, vital, and life-sustaining for me. The mask showed me that the time had come reconcile the part of me who needs to express and the part that has been afraid to be seen and heard. I needed to move from a stance of disavowing the opposing sides of me to a place of reconciling and unifying them. My work with the Guiding Light mask showed me that I was deep in the process of finding my own unique place in the world. It encouraged me to not give up and to trust in my individual destiny, my own "guiding star," to lead the way. The mask came forward as a reminder that finding my true service, aligned with my inner, more integrated Self, should be my chief concern at this time in my life. (Not so ironically, yet surprisingly to me at the time, the mask pointed to my work with masks as being part of my individual destiny, part of my true path of service in this lifetime).

This is where retelling my life story, recasting it for myself in mythopoetic terms, comes in as important. I need to be able to hold my own story without doubt, shame, or apologies, and on the reverse side, without identification or inflation. The work with the Guiding Light mask, and the research and reflection that was initiated by my encounter with the symbols brought me in touch with multilayered, deep-seated issues buried in my inner subterranean realms. Connecting with the glowing, shape-shifting light being embodied in the mask brought comfort as it illuminated the cavernous, abysmal areas of my psyche.

Containing Projections

Creating this first mask in this series engaged imaginal processes whereby I was able to create an external physical object based on an inner experience. By creating the mask, I was able to take the symbols of the guide, the star, and the spark of light outside of myself, enabling the mask to become a container for my psychic projections. I was able to project items out of my unconscious and into the mask.

In donning the mask I was able to begin taking the unconscious material back inward in an embodied way so that I could begin integrating it. The wearing of the mask served to ground the ideas and notions into a physical, somatic experience, thereby turning a symbolic process into a physical and emotional experience. Once this had occurred, I was able to isolate the symbol from the ocean of symbols swelling in my unconscious. I was able to begin working with the symbol consciously, identifying where was it meshed into my personality and initiating the process of separating the psychic material represented by and contained within the symbol, from the *prima materia*.

The deeper illumination came through amplifying the symbols historically. I uncovered an immense amount of material on the guide, the spark of light and the star, but only included in this writing the pieces that were the most relevant to me and my psychological processes at the time of inquiry. The theories of individuation, the Self, and inflation came to the forefront of my attention due to my work with this particular mask.

Contacting the Ineffable

As explained before, the symbol is pointing to something that cannot fully or accurately be represented in the physical realm. It refers to something beyond that which we can grasp with our minds, with our senses, with our reason, or with logic. I again emphasize the importance of personal experience in this work. For me it was: creating the conditions for entering an altered state of consciousness and letting a vibration, an energy move through me, letting an inner force, an archetype arise. My experience is that I set an intention to meet an archetype, to find a meaningful symbol. In order to do this I created a ritual structure, a container in which to invoke non-ordinary states and allowed my unconscious to express itself in what can be most accurately compared, psychologically, to an active imagination. In shamanic terms, I entered an altered state and made contact with the spirit of the mask.

This work has proven to be extremely important to my personal and professional growth. I have spent decades swimming in an ocean of unconscious material, combined with conscious experiences, and external information. It has been intense and overwhelming for me at times. I have sought to sort through the chaos, to find some order, some meaning, in all of my personal *prima materia*. I came into this work intending to distill the first matter so as to transmute it into a higher form, a more refined form.

My process with the two masks, subsequently created, follows a similar course. That which I describe above serves as a blueprint for the masking processes portrayed in the coming chapters.

13 OUT OF DARKNESS

The longing for illumination on the part of those overwhelmed by darkness opens the way, and the journey begins. The shaman and seer drink from the dangerous cup of immortality to know death as life and life as death. What was vulnerable, wounded is now immortalized. ~ Joan Halifax[1]

Mask Two – First Encounters with the Void

From my earlier research, I learned that stars are self-luminous and eventually implode under their own weight. The death of a massive star first creates a supernova shining as bright as a billion suns. It eventually becomes a black hole which produces such an intense gravitational pull that no light can escape.[2] Psychic fragmentation and the resulting sense of deep despair have been described as the alchemical *nigredo*, the blackest black, likened to a black hole. From the ascendant, bright light of the Star, I was plunged into the blackness of the deep space surrounding it. The first mask brought me to the second mask, the Void, which I describe in detail in the following chapters.

Immediately upon completing the basic form of the Guiding Light mask I began having repeated spontaneous visions of a dark mask. The image of a black mask first flashed into my mind during the middle of the day, while I was busy with mundane tasks. With eyes wide open, I saw the mask in front of me as if it were an actual object in my physical world. The black mask appeared to be placed on a chair in my bedroom. It was one of the strangest cross-overs that I can remember of unconscious content merging into my conscious, waking reality. Shortly afterward, I had a dream about an old friend of mine who is a song writer, musician, and a bit of a Trickster. In the dream he was wearing a black mask while engaging in acts of thievery. The dream stayed with me for days. After these two incidents, the image of a black mask began infiltrating my psyche. After some hesitation, I made the decision to consciously begin working with it.

Ritual – Facing the Void

I was tentative and reluctant about working with the dark mask which had repeatedly appeared in my imagination. I sensed shadow material stirring in my psyche every time I thought about the black mask. Just thinking about it brought fear and uncertainty to the point that my stomach literally ached with tension. I have had the experience of unconscious content in the form of memories, intense emotions, and somatic discomforts bursting into my conscious reality unannounced on countless occasions, for decades. I am familiar with the surfacing of the shadow. Fortunately, I have learned how to recognize and contain it before it turns into a destructive internal and external force.

In contemplating the black mask, I immediately recognized the familiar fear that whatever was about to come into consciousness would be too much for me to handle, that it would finally break me apart and shatter me to pieces. I was frightened of what would be shown to me, scared of the shadowy forms reflected in the dark mirror of the black mask. I knew that if I hesitated too long I would get stuck in inertia and fail to create the mask.

I forced myself forward into a ritual, knowing that I had to do something to move the energy out of my psyche, out of my body, lest it sit there under the surface and fester. I knew that if I did not face the unconscious material, it would drop me into melancholy, apathy, and even mild dissociative states, as I have experienced before. I went to my bedroom, lit a candle, and anointed myself with frankincense oil. Frankincense is an ancient oil used as an anointing agent reputed to impart purification and protection to the wearer.[3] I felt like these were qualities I needed to invoke in order to go forward with the ritual and meet this dark one that intimidates me so fundamentally.

After anointing, I lit incense and created a simple altar with statues of the Chinese Goddess of compassion, Kwan Yin, and the Hindu Goddess of death and rebirth, Kali. I imagined a sacred circle surrounding me, summoned comforting psychic figures, and then invited the shadow represented by the mask to be present. I realized, in the moment, that the shadow was already with me. I was simply calling it forward, bringing it fully into consciousness, through the ritual.

As I commenced the ritual, an inner voice said that I know the shadow well. It reminded me that I have done this shadow work many times before and that this is familiar territory. The voice continued, saying that what was new was the conscious act of bringing this material forward. It declared that as a result, I would be able to truly integrate certain aspects of the shadow completely and permanently. It told me that the masked rituals were helping me become more successful and efficient at the same shadow work I had been doing for much of my life.

Following are a few quotes excerpted from the active imagination that occurred in the ritual with the spirit of the soon-to-be-created black mask. I also include a summary of what transpired during my conversation with it. For a complete transcript of the active imagination, see Appendix B. When I invited the spirit behind the black mask to speak, here were the first things it said:

> I am the mystery, yes of death and the great yawning void
> I am not only the unknown, but the absence of the known
> I am a vast emptiness that stretches before you, the emptiness you feared up in space.
> I was there with you and the star.
> We are, in truth, inseparable, the star and I.
> (Azaria, personal journal, April 2010)

The presence went on to challenge me when I asked its permission to create a mask of it and work with it in rituals. It demanded I be certain I was ready to work with it before I created a mask of it. When I hesitated in my answer it reprimanded me: "You'd better be sure…[or else] I will devour you, dismember you. I will rip you to shreds and eat you piece by piece until you become me."

As our dialogue continued, I found the inner voice of this character to be continually questioning and challenging me, as if it did not trust me and my intentions. When I eventually, firmly stated my readiness to work with the energies it represented, the spirit of the mask agreed to be worked with. I asked it again to show me its mask. All I saw was a great, black, gaping void.

Creating Mask Two

I got right to creating the mask, as I was afraid I would be overtaken by my inclination to procrastinate. Instead of thinking it out, or planning the mask in any way, I grabbed a piece of leather and began cutting it while asking the spirit I encountered in the ritual to guide the process. In a trance-like state I cut out the form of the mask with eerie eyes and a big gaping mouth. I quickly began shaping the leather and very rapidly completed the mask. When I was done, I found it to be intense and almost disturbing to look at.

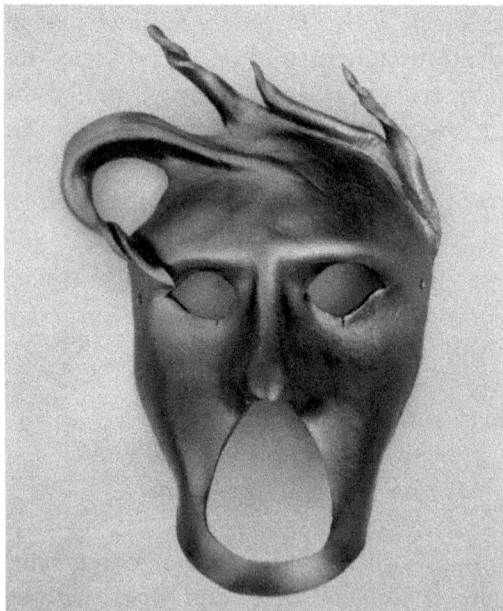

Figure 10: Void Mask

Avoiding the Void

I could not seem to bring myself to paint the Void mask black for quite some time. It sat on my kitchen table for weeks. Every time I approached it, I ended up backing away and distracting myself with other tasks. I was part of the way through creating both of the masks when the process stalled. I scheduled time to work on this masking project, but instead I did house work, chores, errands. I knew it was an avoidance tactic. My conscious self wanted to move forward with this work, yet there was an unconscious block preventing me from doing so.

One afternoon I set aside time to work on my the masks. I could not focus. I did not know where to begin. The idea of getting out all of my painting supplies and equipment overwhelmed me, yet I knew I needed to do something to keep moving the energy if I ever wanted to complete the project.

Releasing Blocks through Art

I could not seem to paint the mask, so I dug through my materials and found four black sheets of paper. I got out my colored pencils, cleared my mind and waited for images to emerge. Quite rapidly they came, one after the other: the void and the star. I created the drawings and then sat with them for a few minutes puzzling over what had emerged on the paper. I did not spend much time with them before putting them away on a shelf.

Several days later I brought them into a therapy session along with my two incomplete masks with the intention of infusing the project with the momentum to keep moving forward. My therapist suggested I sit quietly with the images for a few minutes and see what emerged. As I laid them out, I said that they somehow illustrate a creation myth. I was not sure what that meant, but that is what I kept hearing from an inner voice. Although contemplating the images was uncomfortable, it yielded rich material that helped me reclaim valuable personal assets and understanding that had been buried in the shadows of my unconscious.

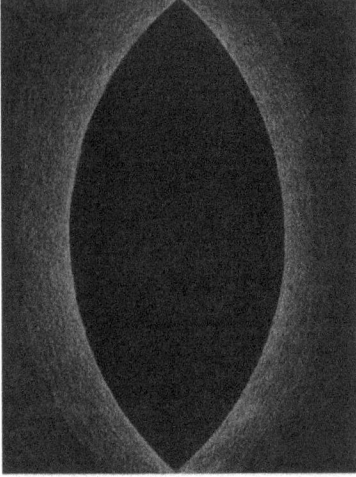

Figure 11. Void 1

Figure 12. Void 2

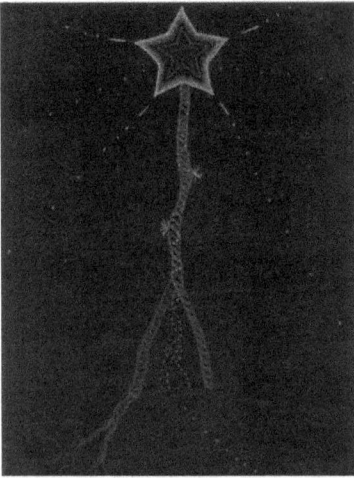

Figure 13. Star 1

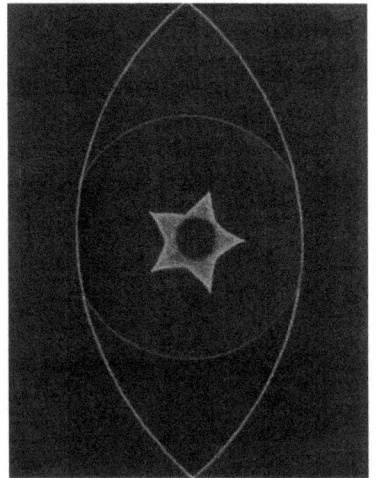

Figure 14. Star 2

Making Associations

As I sat with the four drawings of the void and the star, associations and information began to pour out. The first connection I made was with a mythic story I had recently read of god emptying himself out to create a void in order to bring forth new creation – the manifest world. (I share and cite this myth later in the chapter). This is the necessary act of emptying which precedes the act of creation. The idea of pregnant emptiness is one that is comfortable for me. I can hold it, grasp it, and see the beauty in it. I knew that this was not my block. I knew that I needed to continue circumambulating the symbols. It was still too much for my psyche to take them head on.

I associated image one with the symbol of the *mandorla*. This is the place where two circles join together and form a third space – like an eye or a vulva. In alchemy this symbol represents the place where the opposites unite. It is analogous to the hermetic vessel. The *Mandorla* symbolizes the process Jung termed the transcendent function. Sandplay therapist, Brian Jensen[4] says of this, "The mandorla binds together that which was torn apart and made unwhole-unholy. It is considered the most profound religious experience one can have in life." Also known as the *Vesica Piscis*, it symbolizes the place where opposing worlds and forces interface and interact. It also represents the union of spirit and matter as well as the meeting of heaven and earth.

As I continued to contemplate the drawings, I thought of black holes, which I knew very little about, at the time. What I did know is that they have an intense gravitational pull and that they suck everything in their vicinity into themselves. Black holes let nothing escape, not even light. They are a great cosmic vacuum, the mouth of the primordial devouring void. From the beginning the dark mask reminded me of The Devourer, the Black Hole - sucking life, light, and energy. I associate this idea to complexes that pull things to them with gravitational force, that suck energy, devour libido and hold it in, not letting it escape.

Accessing Pre-verbal States

During the therapy session I found myself frequently at a rare loss for words. It was as if the symbols, and the forces they represent in my psyche, existed in a preverbal state within me. That is why I had to draw them in the first place. I could not yet form words to describe the internal experiences they represent. Since I could not connect words to the images, I felt into my body to see what information was held on a somatic level. I noted my physiological responses to the drawings: I felt a density or compression in my solar plexus and in my throat. I felt fear, anxiety, and tension. I felt my muscles tense slightly. Dropping into the felt experience opened up my psyche and repressed memories began flooding in.

Activating Memory

The darkness I was circumambulating became the darkness of a basement from my childhood, a place where trauma had occurred. I touched into the darkness, into the blackness of the unknown. I dropped into the reality that there are dark regions in my psyche, voids where no memory exists. As I sat with this inner void, I recovered awareness of a childhood fear I had completely dissociated from. In that moment, I began to realize and integrate aspects of my childhood experiences of trauma. My conscious awareness would leave my body during traumatic experiences. I would completely dissociate.

I had known this for decades. But in that moment with the drawings, the awareness of what that experience was *actually like* was illuminated before me. I remembered the sensation clearly for the first time: the fear of leaving my body; the fear of not being able to return; the feeling that I had no control of it and the experience that I can only describe as my soul, spirit, or conscious awareness popping out of my body of its own accord the minute the traumatic event began. While sitting in my therapist's office with the drawings and masks, I could clearly connect the experience of leaving my body as being the early training ground for entering altered states of consciousness and taking what I would later identify as shamanic journeys.

Illuminating the Shadow

Suddenly, I understood the drawing of the star with the ladder. This drawing in particular irritated me. I did not want to draw a cord from the star to the earth, but my psyche insisted. Aesthetically, as an artist, it bothered me from the moment I drew it. After I drew it, I felt it ruined the composition and confused the whole image. At that moment I realized it was an illustration of the mechanism of my dissociation. My soul, my spirit, my conscious self would leave my body and travel up through the darkness of the void, of the vast unknown, and would link to my Star, my Holy Spirit Self. My therapist noted that the star is rooted to the earth - in my drawing, it is firmly grounded.

Through this work I realized that one of the profound gifts of my childhood experience is that I established, at a very early age, a direct link with my Self, with my proverbial Star. This connection kept my psyche safe and intact through all of the complex trauma and subsequent fragmentation. This connection, this ladder to my star, kept me filled with libido or life force energy. It enabled me to stay psychically alive, actively engaged, and able to fully participate in inner and outer life.   It was a vital, life-saving connection. Furthermore, I was able to ground this connection to the Self. Through creative expression, I was able to bring the experience of the Self, and other archetypes, out of my inner depths and into the world through poetry and art. From working with the drawings, I was finally able to finish the Void mask.

It's important to note that this work with the shadow was difficult to approach on my own. I had to use several methods to access it. And I needed to call on the expert help of a guide, in the form of my therapist, to help me navigate this dark and painful terrain. I have found that this work is quite potent and quite real. I caution those who wish to engage in it to take it very seriously and to make sure the proper containment and support systems are in place for you and any students you may work with. While the results are incredible, and even uncanny, the process can be difficult and can activate wound material that needs to be carefully navigated. This should be kept in mind whenever engaging in mask work or any other techniques that directly address and activate the unconscious.

End Notes

1. Halifax, 1982, p. 26
2. Ronnberg & Martin, 2010
3. Essential Science Publishing, 2000
4. Jensen, 2001

14 ENTER THE VOID

While the work with the Void was difficult, it proved to be incredibly illuminating and healing. With the realization of how my trauma activated shamanic experiences and brought me into direct contact with my own guiding spirit – the Self - came a whole other set of associations. I continued exploring ideas surrounding the four void and star drawings, based on previous knowledge and research.

I immediately thought of Seshet, the Egyptian goddess represented with the line coming out of her head, attached to a seven-pointed star. (I discovered her when researching the Star). She is the only female depicted as engaged in the act of writing within all of Egyptian art. She is the sole female scribe and the wife of Thoth.[1] As I contemplated this ancient Egyptian goddess, I began to see how Sehsat correlates with the part of me, the part of my Star-Self, that is and has always been a scribe, diligently recording experiences and impressions. I had recently wrote about my scribe qualities many months before I created the drawings and before I knew anything about Seshat. I felt, in that moment, that some of the archetypes and symbols I had been working with were finally beginning to interconnect in a meaningful way. It was very exciting.

The next thought that came to me was something I had read on Kwan Yin going down into hell to feed the demons and devils. I had recently read about how she cloaks herself to do this (as did my own Guide, the Star) and how there is a string coming out the top of her head connecting her to her higher self, which I explain below. The synchronicities and symbols were beginning to disentangle so that the mass of confusion, the *prima materia,* was beginning to differentiate into clear and applicable psychic descriptors that were greatly informing my personal process.

Amplifying the Archetypes and Symbols - The Void

The Void and Emptying

A void, by definition, is an empty space, a vacuum, an opening, a gap, an absence, a hollowness.[2] *Kenosis* is a Greek word for emptying.[3] The idea of kenosis comes from an ancient notion that every month the moon voluntarily empties herself of light. She darkens as she moves toward the sun, which now holds the light she has poured out. Jung points out that this process of emptying parallels the kenosis doctrine of the church, which basically says that "[T]he incarnation of Christ took place through a voluntary process of emptying: he emptied himself of his divinity in order to become man."[4] It is similar to the bodhisattva tradition which Kwan Yin personifies. Jung[5] says of this:

> [Kwannon, the Goddess of Kindness] gives nourishment to all living beings, even to the evil spirits in hell, and to do so she must go down to hell; but it will frighten the devils if she were to appear there in her heavenly form and, as the Goddess of Kindness, she cannot permit that to happen; so, having such an extraordinary regard for the feelings of the devils, she transforms herself into the guise of an evil spirit and takes the food down in that guise. There is a beautiful traditional painting where she is represented in hell as a devil among the devils, giving them food; but there is a fine thread going up from her head to a heavenly being above, who is herself in all her splendid fury.

According to Edinger[6], this image of Kwan Yin in hell is a way of expressing the assimilation of the shadow. Her willingness to take the form of an evil spirit in order to feed the evil spirits in hell is another example of kenosis. She empties herself in order to nourish the shadow. Another example of the concept of kenosis is the Kabbalistic doctrine of Tisimtsum. It is the idea that god had to empty a part of himself in order to make room for creation. This passage quoted in Edward Edinger's book[7] on the alchemical *mysterium coniunctio* (union of opposites) explains the necessity of the process:

> It means...that the existence of the universe is made possible by a process of shrinkage in God...If God is "all in all," how can there be things which are not God? How can God create the world out of nothing, if there is no nothing?...God was compelled to make room for the world by, as it were, abandoning a region within Himself, a kind of mystical primordial space from which He withdrew in order to return to it in the act of creation and revelation.

This, basically, is idea of the creative void. It is the idea that nothing new can emerge until an empty space is made for it. Emptying is the precursor to creating. Edinger says we all start out identifying with god; we are the center of our universe, we are one with the god image, we are merged and think ourselves omnipotent. Then, we go through a "lengthy, laborious process of emptying that original state of identification..." in order to develop a conscious ego that is aware of its limitations.[8] The ego has to dis-identify with the Self, which is to go through the alchemical process of *separatio*, or separation, in order to unite with the Self in a transformative *coniunctio*.

The void has been compared to the original state of the unconscious before it has been differentiated. Israeli Jungian analyst and author, Erel Shalit[9] makes an interesting connection between the unconscious and its relationship to the void in the following quote:

> [The undifferentiated unconscious] is the original chaos, the undifferentiated, formless void we hear about at the very beginning of Genesis (1:2) where it says that 'the earth was without form, and void.' This is the Hebrew *tohu* and *bohu*, which etymologically are related to emptiness and chaos, nothingness and confusion, amazement and going astray.

The focus of individuation is the separating and clarifying of unconscious material so that it can be reintegrated into conscious awareness. The starting point is always the original state of chaos symbolized as the formless, undifferentiated void.

The Void and Zero

The void, as a consummate symbol of emptiness, represents unimaginable potential which affiliates it with the mystery and power or the number zero. In the Hindu tradition, zero represents the great emptiness, the quality-less layer of existence that rests behind all of creation.[10] The Hindu root of the word zero, *vi*, connotes the pregnant void, the swelling receptive womb which holds the potential to birth forth all things from its emptiness.[11] The potency of zero comes through with expansive and profound implications that defy our ability to understand and articulate. The ARAS Book of Symbols[12] has a succinct description of the power of zero:

> [W]hile a frightening reminder of the primal void, zero has both logic-defying mathematical properties and the power to suggest the abyss of infinity...Modern physics has discovered zero is its own portal to the infinite, with absolute zero the theoretical freezing point of all molecular movement, the zero space of the black hole, the limitless zero point energy of quantum mechanic's vacuum and the cosmic zero of the big bang theory, the cataclysmic creation of the universe from nothingness...In a psychic sense, zero holds all the terrors of nullity, nonexistence and death.

In a social sense, being a "zero" is like being a complete non-entity, existing in a social void. While this is a cruel and inaccurate projection usually associated with adolescent ideas, the idea is that, in the human social realm, a "zero" is relegated to non-existence. This is the converse of existing. To not exist is to essentially be dead. In the end, death is the ultimate unknown which awaits us all. In this way zero, representing the great nothingness of the void, appears as a threshold to the unknown and the unimaginable.

The Void and Death

As described above, the concept of the void is comparable to zero, the great nothing, absolute nullity, and the vast, gaping emptiness of the cosmos. It represents the end of the known and as such, is connected to death. Death is a mysterious, often terrifying, altogether unknown reality that lurks on the border of conscious awareness and unconscious denial. Fear of death is an innate part of our biology. If our survival instincts move us towards life, it follows that they would also move us away from death.

The dark mask, with its messages of facing the vast unknown of the void, served as a reminder that death is the inescapable partner of life. Together these forces represent the energies of creation and destruction that underlie all existence. These are the great and terrible opposites that, in the end, we all must face and integrate if we can ever hope for psychic wholeness. Dionysus, God of the Mask, was associated with the paradox of the intrinsic connection between life and death, creation and destruction. Walter Otto, in his seminal tome *Dionysus: Myth and Cult* illuminates the Dionysian polarity:

> We know him as the wild spirit of antithesis and paradox, of immediate presence and complete remoteness, of bliss and horror, of infinite vitality and cruelest destruction. The element of bliss in his nature, the creative, enraptured, and blessed elements all share, too, in his wildness and his madness. Are they not, then, mad just because they, too, already carry within themselves a duality, because they stand on the threshold where one step beyond leads to dismemberment and darkness? Here we have hit upon a cosmic enigma – the mystery of life which is self-generating, self-creating...He who begets something which is alive must dive down into the primeval depths in which the forces of life dwell. And when he rises to the surface, there is a gleam of madness in his eyes because in those depths death lives cheek by jowl with life. The primal mystery is itself mad – the matrix of the duality and the unity of disunity.[13]

Aside from the literal, final death which ushers us out of life in a body, we undergo numerous psychological and emotional deaths throughout a lifetime. It is a common occurrence that, at some point in midlife, the course of inner development of an individual falls out of sync with the conscious attitude of the ego. There is a conflict between opposing inner and outer forces that, with a change of attitude, can lead to growth. This type of growth often requires a death of certain aspects of the ego. A letting go must occur so that new life can emerge in harmony with the growth required. Again, this is the alchemical *nigredo,* the state of break-down, of death and decay. If it is resisted, depression and other undesirable psychological and emotional consequences can arise. We will inevitably suffer from our own imbalanced psyche.[14]

Death is the precursor to new life, just as emptiness is the antecedent of creation. The current state must be emptied and released in order for a new state to enter. The old must die before the new can be born. This is the alchemical *nigredo,* also known as the *motificatio.*[15] As Otto[16] explains, to beget new life, one must descend into the depths where life originates and in so doing, come face to face with death. Entry into the shadow lands of death is a pivotal phase in the journey of initiation. I believe the dark mask arrived to usher me into the initiatory descent into darkness.

End Notes

1. Wilkinson, 2003
2. Merriam-Webster, 1973
3. Edinger, 1994
4. Edinger, 1994, p. 44
5. Jung, as cited in Edinger, 1994, p. 46
6. Edinger, 1994
7. Edinger, 1994, p. 46
8. Edinger, 1994, p. 46
9. Shalit, 2008, p. 91
10. Ronnberg & Martin, 2010
11. Ronnberg & Martin, 2010
12. Ronnberg & Martin, 2010, p. 708
13. Otto, 1965, p. 136-137
14. Jung, 1959; Von Franz, 1974
15. Edinger, 1991
16. Otto, 1965

15 INITIATORY DESCENT

My work with the Void mask pointed me in the direction of initiatory descent. The story of the descent into darkness is as widespread as it is ancient. There are numerous myths to turn to when seeking a map into the darker territory of psychic initiation. The masks pointed the way to Dionysus, god of the mask as an initiating force.

When I looked into the ancient well of Dionysian mythology, I found that the story of his union with Ariadne was a thread worth following. As I began researching, I found that this particular myth guided the mysterious initiation rites of women in western antiquity for hundreds, perhaps thousands, of years.

I had already done some work with the initiatory myths of Inanna, ancient Sumerian "Queen of the Heavens," and her dark, underworld counter-part, Ereshkigal, and I had been exploring the myth of Sophia, the spark of light who descended or "fell" from the heavens to be trapped in matter and undergo an initiatory redemption process. But when the myth of Dionysus and Ariadne's alchemical union crossed my path, it was the clear and obvious choice of direction.[1]

Breaking it Down

The initial stage of psychological initiation involves moving away from the world of ego consciousness and dropping into the inner realm of unconscious material, represented by the descent into darkness. This is followed by the breaking apart of rigid ego structures, represented by dismemberment and death. This phase of the initiation process is mirrored in the myth of Ariadne and Dionysus, as I explain below.

In initiatory myths the protagonist (the hero or heroine) has a catastrophic collision with powerful external forces. The collision initiates a fall into darkness which entails a stripping away of the former light-based (conscious) identity. The heroine must confront dangerous forces symbolized as the powers of death, destruction, and decay. These symbols embody the psychological forces that eat away at conscious, death-denying attitudes. They break apart the rigid structures of consciousness, grinding them down to an essential state that can then be digested and transformed. The destructive powers of initiation are akin to the *nigredo* phase in alchemy, the descent into darkness, the death of the old form which always precedes the birth of the new.[2] This is the point in initiation, in individuation, and in alchemy when the previous creation must be destroyed and returned to the chaotic state of the void, the *prima materia*, before a new creation can occur. This is the act of emptying that precedes creation.

In psychological terms this is the dismantling of ego-defenses and identifications. It is a peeling away of the beliefs, often faulty and resulting from wounds, which nevertheless serve as the foundation holding us in place in the external world. Psychological death is an essential part of the initiation process and it is extremely unsettling and disorienting.

The Myth of Ariadne and Dionysus

Ariadne's story mirrors the process of transformation as it occurred in ancient women's mystery rites, a process that aligns with modern descriptions of individuation. Ariadne was said to be the daughter of the mythical king of Crete, Minos and his wife Pasiphae, who were linked to the symbols of the bull and the cow, respectively. Before Ariadne was born, Pasiphae mated with a wild bull, producing the Minotaur who was subsequently locked away into the center of the legendary Cretan labyrinth.[3] Ariadne and her sister Phaedra, conceived within the marriage and born much later, are portrayed as having opposite yet complementary characteristics.

It is important to note that in some versions of her myth, Ariadne, "Mistress of the Labyrinth," is betrothed to Dionysus from the beginning of the story. In other versions, Dionysus sees Ariadne on the isle of Naxos and immediately falls in love with her.[4] Either way, the sacred union between the two of them, which I describe in Chapter Nineteen, is at the heart of the ancient mystery traditions of the Mediterranean region.[5]

Ariadne's parents, as bull and cow, represent the undifferentiated, primeval forces of the unconscious.[6] They represent the chaotic state of the *prima materia* before it has been differentiated. With Ariadne and Phaedra, the opposites clearly diverge for the first time. Psychologically speaking, Phaedra belongs solely to the world of light, the world of consciousness and the ego. Ariadne is connected with the underworld realms of the unconscious and in this way, is said to belong to both the mortal world *and* the world of the gods. Ariadne's infamous thread guides the hero Theseus to the center of the underworld labyrinth, where he slays the Minotaur, and then leads him back to the upper world of civilized Crete[7].

Turning Away from Soul

It is here where Ariadne transgresses, which ultimately leads her to the death that brings rebirth. She "belongs" to Dionysus in his form as the bull god, but she falls in love with Theseus, the Athenian hero whom she helps to destroy her half-brother, the Minotaur. When he promises to marry her, she runs off with Theseus to Athens. The entry of Theseus into her story represents the dawning of the light of consciousness. Ariadne becomes attracted to the qualities of consciousness embodied by Theseus which include worldly, masculine, heroic attributes. She gives herself over entirely to the world of consciousness and, in so doing, rejects the darkness of her origin and the spark of light (represented by Dionysus) that exists in the depths. This implies that the unconscious and the soul are repressed by the ego's desire for consciousness alone. Mythologically, consciousness is often represented as the male hero and the unconscious is said to be feminine. The unconscious is widely held as the Great Mother, the primal void from which the psyche of both women and men, originates.[8] Fierz-David describes the implications of Ariadne following the hero and rejecting her deep origins:

Thus Ariadne loses contact with the light that is concealed in the earth and has always ruled her, represented here by Dionysus as the bull, who embodies the creative force of the emotions…She hurries beyond herself toward the light of the world (Athens) in order to be one-sidedly conscious.[9]

When Ariadne betrays her connection to Dionysus and the chthonic world, she meets with disaster. In one version, her journey with Theseus is thwarted by Artemis, the feminine moon-like principle which does not abide the one-sidedness of masculine (yang) oriented consciousness. Artemis bewitches Ariadne and makes her as "one who is sleeping," represented by the image of Ariadne falling asleep on the isle of Naxos where she is thus abandoned by Theseus (who in some versions runs off with her sister – the all-conscious Phaedra). Theseus, the embodiment of consciousness, leaves her there.

Hitting Bottom

In great despair, Ariadne hangs herself on the isle of Naxos, where she awaits the embrace of death. She falls into utter hopelessness, which is the turning point in the myth. At the pinnacle of complete darkness and desolation, Ariadne surrenders herself to death. The image of hanging oneself is a harrowing representation of a complete and deliberate release of life itself. This personal sacrifice brings in Dionysus, in the form of the god of death, a form he was known to occupy along with his more well-known attributes.[10] The rest of the myth is examined in Chapter Nineteen, where I illuminate the psychological implications of the mystical, transformational union that occurs at this point in the story.

It is only through falling into darkness and suffering the pain of wounding that Ariadne is able to induce in herself the conditions for redemption and restoration that come with Dionysus' appearance. It is in the depths of the darkness and suffering that Ariadne submits to the powers of death in order to be transformed and recreated anew. In accord with the concept of kenosis, Ariadne empties herself of life itself in order to be transformed.

The dark mask, symbol of the Void, brought me to a place of emptying the ego constructs that had been defending me against acknowledging my own wounds. My work with the mask brought me to a threshold where I was plunged into darkness that revealed itself as a deep sense of emotional devastation. Because of the opening created by my work with the masks, I had the wherewithal to spend months in a place of internal darkness, sitting with my wounds and letting them tell me their stories.

The Wound

The wound, rooted in the Latin word *vulnus,* (related to the word vulnerable), is typically the result of trauma.[11] Wounds represent tears, holes, and injuries both visible and invisible. To be wounded is to have our vulnerabilities and our mortality revealed and exposed.[12] In mythic terms the wound is an opening in the very fabric of reality which becomes a portal to transformation. Stories of transformative wounding are found across times and cultures. Throughout history neither gods nor goddesses; men nor women have been exempt from the realities of wounding. Wounds can act as initiatory passageways, dropping one down into deep places where numinous experiences realign our relationship to ourselves and the world. Through the experience of woundedness, new aspects of being surface and come to light.[13]

Psychoanalysis relies, in part, on techniques that uncover the wounds of past, repressed trauma. By going into the areas of woundedness, one frees up libido (life energy) which has been stuck at the site of the injury and which has been siphoned off to keep the cycle of repression in place. The process of uncovering, cleansing and healing psychic wounds can be delicate and dangerous work, requiring an emptying of the ego structures that keep us away from these dark and painful places. Wounds are often buried deeply in the unconscious and can be difficult to access. Sigmund Freud[14] illuminated the process of burying trauma through the mechanism of repression. Repression is insidious and demanding. It requires an ongoing outlay of energy to keep the repression in place. Of this Freud says:

> The process of repression is not to be regarded as an event which takes place once, the results of which are permanent. Repression demands a persistent expenditure of force, and if this were to cease the success of the repression would be jeopardized, so that a fresh act of repression would be necessary.[15]

Eventually, too many cracks in the ego-structure can rupture the cycle of repression. The hidden wounds surface and healing transformation is set in motion.

Wounded Healer

From his extensive cross-cultural studies, ethnopsychologist Holger Kalweit (1984) has linked the phenomena of death, illness, wounding, and suffering with the mysterious healing abilities of indigenous shamans worldwide. He notes that the power to heal others often results from the shamanic practitioner first undergoing a process of injury and suffering, followed by purification and healing which facilitates the acquisition of the tools and skills required in healing. He describes psychic and physical suffering as "...a means of altering consciousness and as forces and mechanisms of transformation and self-healing."[16] Through the destructive forces of injury and wounding, the forces of healing and repair are released.

The Wound in Mythology

Wounds are often the doorway to the adventure of initiation and transformation in myths and stories. Of the hundreds of examples available, I have selected a few to mention as illustration. Osiris and Dionysus were dismembered; Prometheus suffered the continual rending of his liver by Zeus's eagle; the Fisher King of the Grail saga was driven by his wound; Job was punished with boils; Jesus was nailed to the cross. The stories of feminine wounding are so plentiful that they seem, to me, to be core themes in feminine mythology. Medusa was first raped and then beheaded; Sedna was mutilated and then cast to the bottom of the sea; and Hathor was abducted and raped for performing healing acts.[17] Through the powers of the wound, that which is buried in the darkness of the individual and collective unconscious is delivered into consciousness and thereby liberated. As the great poet Rumi said: "The wound is the place where the Light enters you."

Walking Wounded

It is important to mention that, although filled with transformative potential, psychological wounding does not always lead to healing, liberation, and empowerment. There are many stages to the alchemical transformation of a personality and if any of them are skipped over or abandoned prematurely, successful initiation fails to occur. For reasons that differ from person to person, the resultant shadow material that surrounds the phenomenon of wounding is not always brought forward for deliberate contemplation. Or when it is, it is not always thoroughly separated and refined so that it can be reunited into a new state of wholeness. If the unconscious material is not appropriately contained and integrated, the result is an individual who does *not* experience restoration, but instead remains fragmented and exhibits it as one of the so-called "walking wounded."

The Sacrifice

The word sacrifice has obvious connections with the word sacred. The dictionary defines sacrifice as: "[A]n act of offering to a deity something precious; the killing of a victim on an altar; destruction or surrender of something for the sake of something else; something given up or lost."[18] In mythology and religion the one who is sacrificed often becomes a redeemer. Take for example the stories of Jesus and of Dionysus, two figures whom underwent sacrificial death to later emerge as redeeming forces.

The archetype of sacrifice transcends the social constructs of the human world. One only has to look at the natural world to see the cycle of predator and prey, devourer and devoured, embedded in the dance of life. Every day, life in one form or another is sacrificed so that other life can be sustained. Humans did not invent the concept of sacrifice, yet it is likely that we have struggled with it for millennia, causing the subject of sacrifice to be relegated to the shadow realms of the personal and collective unconscious. My work with the black mask opened up the notion of sacrifice for further contemplation.

It seems that, in order to transform, we must be willing to sacrifice, to let go and leap into the void of the unknown. In the initiatory myth, Ariadne surrendered her own life in hopes of transcending the pain and remorse that was devouring her.

During my work with the dark mask questions emerged from my unconscious that begged for a deeper level of self-reflection:

- What parts of me, of my ego and persona, am I willing to sacrifice?
- What deeply entrenched beliefs am I willing to give up?
- What parts of my conscious identity am I ready to let go of and let die so that something new can emerge?

I began realizing that there were naïve parts of me, parts that had been wounded and that were blocking progress in certain areas of my life. I began realizing that perhaps it was time to further release pieces of my personal story of wounding.

Other questions followed:

- What about aspects of me that I sacrificed, consciously and unconsciously, that needed to be redeemed and restored in order to achieve wholeness?
- What about parts of me that have already undergone death and decay and are seeking rebirth?

My work with the dark mask helped me see that it was time to give all of these parts of myself space to come forward into my conscious awareness.

The Scapegoat

The one being sacrificed is often the scapegoat. In ancient Greece, goats were sacrificed to Dionysus, god of tragedy, which translates as the "goat song" from the Greek *tragos,* meaning goat.

The idea behind Greek tragedy originated with the Dionysian dythrambic satyr play.[19] The goat, representing unconscious lustful and aggressive drives, is a fitting symbol for Dionysus, god of unbound passion who was known to stir the civilized hero to the brink of madness. The civilized person's fear of such unbridled passions has accounted, in part, for the goat's classification as evil. The mixture of independence, rowdy behavior, and intense sex-drive combined with the goat's otherworldly eyes and appearance, have led to the Judeo-Christian projection of evil, in fact, of the very devil, onto the goat.[20] The goat has been symbolically linked with darkness and untamed carnal passion. In Christian and Judaic lore, illness, shame, and sin could be magically transferred onto the goat which would then be banished to the wilds as the scapegoat.

Scapegoating is a worldwide phenomenon. It is archetypal. In ancient times the scapegoat was an animal or human sacrificed to appease the destructive forces personified as the gods of death and the underworld. In this way the scapegoat was a healing agent and the sacrifice was a death that had profound meaning attached to it.[21] It served as a collective reminder of the ambiguous forces of creation and destruction which rule the temporal world. The scapegoat provides a sacred service in its sacrifice, which Author and Jungian analyst Silvia Brinton Perera[22] implores us to remember:

> The scapegoat was a pharmakon or healing agent. In the scapegoat rituals it was dedicated to and identified with the god. It functioned to bring the transpersonal dimension to aid and renew the community, for the community acknowledged that it was embedded in and dependent on transpersonal forces. The scapegoat ritual, like others, was used 'to enrich meaning or call attention to other levels of existence…[I]t incorporate[d] evil and death along with life and goodness into a single, grand, unifying pattern.'

In psychology, the idea of scapegoating has many meanings. For instance, in family systems, the scapegoat is the one who carries the projections of failure, weakness and shame for the other members of the family.[23] Within depth psychology, scapegoating is a way of denying the shadow in both humans and the divine and can take place within the interior of one's own psyche.[24] That which threatens or opposes the ego's ideas of human and divine goodness and rightness is deemed corrupt and evil and is vanquished. Psychological scapegoating inhibits creative psychological growth, for conscious apprehension of the shadow pollinates creative impulses, spurs individuation, and deepens our ability to connect and relate.[25]

Embracing Ambivalence

The reality that the natural world, and perhaps even life itself is founded on ambivalent forces, forces equally capable of helping us or harming us, can be a frightening and painful thing to realize. Historically, rites and rituals helped to make these dark realities more endurable for our ancestors. It seems that my personal rites with the masks were helping me integrate painful realities of the world and of my personal life history, rendering them both more endurable.

In my opinion, the realization that our world is founded on ambiguous forces, which are as good as they are bad, is pivotal to spiritual maturation. The naive longing for the world to be good and fair is replaced by the stark awakening that dynamic polarity underlies the world's very existence. Jung speaks of the inherent duality of the Old Testament creator God: "Yaweh is not split, but is an antimony – a totality of inner opposites – and this is the indispensable condition for his tremendous dynamism."[26] From a mythological perspective, creation springs from the dynamic tension that arises from the polarization of the opposites. It is this same dynamic tension between destruction and creation, between death and rebirth that leads to the creation of the individuated personality.

End Notes

1. Fierz-David, 1980; Hall, 1988
2. Edinger, 1991
3. Fierz-David, 1980; Kerenyi, 1976; Wilkinson, 2010
4. Fierz-David, 1980; Kerenyi, 1976; Wilkinson, 2010
5. Fierz-David, 1980; Kerenyi, 1976
6. Fierz-David, 1980
7. Fierz-David, 1980; Kerenyi, 1976; Wilkinson, 2010
8. Neumann, 1969
9. Fierz-David, 1980, p. 24
10. Kerenyi, 1976; Otto, 1965
11. Ronnberg & Martin, 2010
12. Ronnberg & Martin, 2010
13. Leonard, 1982; Ronnberg & Martin, 2010; Shalit, 2008
14. Freud, 1989
15. Freud, 1989, p. 572
16. Kalweit, 1984, p. 75
17. Wilkinson, 2009
18. Merriam-Webster, 1973
19. Ronnberg & Martin, 2010
20. Ronnberg & Martin, 2010
21. Perera, 1986
22. Perera, 1986, p. 8
23. Coleman, 1996
24. Perera, 1986; Ronnberg & Martin, 2010
25. Coleman, 1996; Perera, 1986; Ronnberg & Martin, 2010
26. Jung, 1957, p. 7

16 RECLAIMING THE REJECTED

Shadow and the Awakening Self

Jung described the Self as the totality of the psyche which unites the opposites and holds everything, including the ego and the shadow, together in balance and unity. He believed that the path of individuation unfolds differently for each person and that the archetypal Self is the only true guide we can hope for in seeking authentic spiritual and psychological unfolding.[1]

Sexual desire, aggression, envy, and hate are shame-producing emotions and these normal human reactions are hidden away in embarrassment into the shadow regions.[2] Shadow integration is the process of getting to know and accept the parts of ourselves we have felt shameful about. It is a coming to terms with the parts of us that are deemed unacceptable and are rejected by the ego and persona.[3] To approach a state of wholeness, we must welcome back the parts that have been cut off. Wholeness means allowing and accepting the whole of us, shadow and all.

It seems that my psyche has been pointing me towards an understanding of the Self archetype, represented by the Guiding Light mask, and its relationship to the shadow, represented by the Void mask. My work, thus far, seemed to indicate that I was in an initiation phase of the individuation process aimed at differentiating my inner shadow and integrating it into my conscious identity.

Entering the Unknown

At one point during my work with the masks, I became saturated and exhausted from the intense material that was surfacing. I felt as if progress started slowing and like I was circumambulating the same old wounds over and over again. Knowing from my depth studies that it is part of the process, I sincerely tried to surrender and accept where I was at. My ego was challenged by the state of emptiness and by the unknown horizons presented by the masks. It was uncomfortable not knowing what my next steps in the journey were going to be or when they were going to show up. The intense inner polarizing dynamics of wanting to open and close, to stay present to the work and to split off at the same time, were leaving me with little energy.

Getting Lost

Because the narrative of psychic development reveals itself over time in an indirect, often irrational manner, it can be challenging for the conscious mind of the ego to follow its movement. Suddenly, I found myself feeling lost in the process to the point that I could not even articulate where I was in it. The only thing to do at a time like this is to watch for signs and open to information coming from the unconscious mind in the form of dreams, visions, art, and so forth. Jung and von Franz would agree that the best thing to do when arriving at an impasse in an initiation phase of individuation is to seek guidance from the Self. Von Franz[4] advises:

> If the ego could relate directly to the Self, which is a unifying symbol, the conflict would fade and the ego would function again in wholeness. That is the normal way in which the opposites function, and the main impulse is again the flow of life, the ego serving or moving along the flow of life which comes from the totality. A conflict is never really solved, but the emotion invested in it diminishes, one outgrows it by suffering, and it becomes absorbed in a new form of life, with the result that one looks back dispassionately on it from a different angle.

Tension Between Opposites

As the tension of internal opposites reaches a climax, there is much discomfort and a state of suspension can arise where everything seems stuck in inexplicable inertia. The ego doesn't know which way to go and forward movement is arrested. This is a difficult state to hold, but it is a necessary part of transformation. For a time, I abandoned my work with the masks as I experienced the previous sense of clarity dissolving into a state of chaos and confusion. Ultimately, in this situation, the ego must surrender and realize that it cannot solve the conflict on its own. It must relinquish the illusion that it is in control and submit to something larger than itself. It must surrender to the numinous inner guide, the Self. I believe the masks were guiding me to this place of surrender, to which I finally succumbed.

Facing Duality

Through my work with the Void mask, I came to see that I was undergoing an initiation into the mysteries of the dual nature of the manifest world. My persona had cracked and fallen away, my ego was being tossed about by unconscious forces, and I was in the process of slowly differentiating the many facets of my shadow. I had been actively, consciously working with the same personal and collective wounds for over two decades. Yet embodying the emptiness, the darkness, the death and annihilation of the Void, through the mask, brought an eruption of buried emotion and with it an *embodied understanding* of the devastation caused by the early wounding of the feminine principle experienced in the traumas of my childhood. The clarity of understanding that emerged solidified a profound compassion for the parts of me that have suffered immensely and which have, subsequently, been banished to the shadows.

Through the work done thus far, I started to differentiate the various aspects and layers of shadow material in my psyche. I began to recognize the presence of primitive emotions in my shadow that embody the duality of the natural world, such as the predator and the prey; the creator and the destroyer. Through mask work, I was facing the destructive forces in my own psyche which were blocking forward progress in certain areas of my life. Through my work with the dark mask I began to recognize the archetypal nature of the forces of destruction and to come to terms with their place in the cycle of life. I started to understand that Destruction is an archetypal figure within each of us that is intrinsically bound to the archetype of Creation. When we deny the destructive force, it goes into the shadow and is then projected out into the world where it is disowned and seen as completely other. When this happens, the internal pattern of death-destruction and rebirth-creation is stunted.

In my personal journey with the masks, I entered the shadow realms of my unconscious - the realms of darkness, death, and rot – with the intention of further healing the fragmentation in my psyche caused by the push and pull of opposing forces. I entered seeking a way out of the polarization of the opposites I was struggling with at the time: introversion vs. extraversion, feminine qualities of being (yin) vs. masculine qualities of doing (yang), and the parts of me that seek expression vs. the parts of me that want to hide.

Embracing Vulnerability

I have suffered from shame around my history of trauma. The shame has sometimes prevented me from sharing my creative work which addresses personal and collective wounds. I have experienced internal conflict between the parts of me that wish to share my work and the parts of me that wish to withhold it. The conflict results in a stalemate which had kept much of my creative work sitting dusty on a shelf for years. When the inner conflict is activated, I find myself frozen and unable to move forward. My work with the Light and Void masks began to loosen the knot of unconscious material that had been tied up around sharing art and writing that has emerged from the deep places of wounding within me.

Through engaging the Void mask my own psyche demanded that I drop defensive pretenses and expose the fragile, wounded aspects of my being in order to continue healing from the many traumatic experiences I lived through. It was very humbling to return to a place of utter vulnerability. Through the course of my work with the black mask, there came a stark realization that something within me needed to be sacrificed in order to free up enough libido to support the new life that was trying to emerge. Throughout the process I continued challenging myself to stand firm and confront my own inner darkness and face my own shadowy fears, like facing the Minotaur at the center of the labyrinth. From studying the initiation myths, I knew that each step was preparing me to confront my own inner beast of darkness and death who would just as soon destroy me as offer me new life.

The Reconciling Third

The need to transcend the opposites and find a new, third way – like the *transcendent function* in alchemy, which can hold the opposites in balance and harmony - rose to the forefront of my psyche[5]. During my work with the Void mask, it became clear that a third mask would be coming to help reconcile the conflict between the light (Star) and the dark (Void). My work with the Star, representing my unique individual destiny, and the Void, representing the obstacles set in motion by suffering primal wounding, were reaching climactic tension. I knew something needed to come along to shift the inertia created by the opposing forces clashing against each other. I also knew that it was not something I could force. I knew that, in order for it to be authentic and truly effective, it had to arise from a place much deeper than my conscious mind has access to. Like the Star and the Void, the third mask had to arise from the unconscious in its own way and its own time.

Surrender to the Mystery

I had to come to the realization that I could not use my will to control or force the process. The process is beyond me. I knew that it has its own timing and would reach a conclusion in due course. And I knew that I would have to somehow mark the transition back into the world and bring back the gifts of the darkness. The process is not complete until I enter the world in a new way and bring the wisdom of the transformation to my community. This is the *rubedo* phase in alchemy, the completion of a cycle, when the *lapis* – the goal of the transformation – is reached.[6]

At this point in the process, I had minimal understanding of Ariadne's progression from self-sacrifice to a state of redemption and restoration, yet I had to trust that the masks themselves would guide me to a place of understanding. Although at this stage I was still immersed in the mystery, I trusted that I would emerge more fully intact, vital, and whole from the initiatory experiences activated by the masks.

Lighting the Darkness

According to Jung[7], the guiding star leads one through the darkness of the unknown. He describes the appearance of the star symbol in psyche as the moment we realize that we are not in control of life, the moment we understand that despite our ability to make choices, we are ultimately under the influence of an "unknown will with an unknown design" which sweeps us each along our life course. As he so wisely proclaimed: "One does not become enlightened by imagining figures of light, but by making the darkness conscious."

In the coming chapters I examine the culminating phase of the initiation process, (the further clarification of opposites), followed by the mysterious union of opposites which yields the unified personality (the alchemical gold). We'll continue with the next stages of the myth of Ariadne and Dionysus and meet the third and final mask in the series.

End Notes

1. Jung, 1959
2. Stein, 1998
3. Stein, 1998
4. Von Franz, 1974, p. 38
5. Edinger, 1991
6. Edinger, 1991
7. Jung, 1945, p. 335

17 AWAKENING INSTINCTS

The difference between being born and the births occurring later in life is the awareness of your ignorance – that you know you cannot know what is coming. ~Nor Hall[1]

Creating Mask Three – Trickster Style

The creation of the third mask came unexpectedly while I was on a trip visiting a friend on California's Central Coast. On the evening of my arrival I pulled a card from her MotherPeace Tarot deck as we drank tea and chatted in her living room. I pulled card 0, The Fool, which is related to the beginning and the end as well as to the Trickster[2]. It was the first time I had pulled a card other than the Star for many months. I wondered if this was an indication of a shift in my psyche. I found the card quite apropos, for I had met this woman the previous summer when we both presented our work on the relationship between Trickster, art and healing at an international shamanic conference. I noted the card in my journal and then forgot about it.

During my four day visit we talked a lot about art, Trickster, carnival, and Dionysus. We had planned to do art-making at some point during my trip. When my friend learned that I make leather masks, she wanted me to teach her. Trickster was afoot throughout the process. It was as if the moment we decided to make masks together the archetypal force swept in and took us for a ride. The entire creation process was rife with Trickster dynamism. To begin, my friend wanted to visit her local leather craftsman to purchase leather, perhaps borrow tools, and see if he had any useful tips for us. I had described for her the process I had successfully followed numerous times, but she seemed to be in pursuit of further knowledge. I welcome adventure, so I agreed to join her investigation. The visit to the leather shop yielded the purchase of some nice leather pieces and an antiquated article on leather sculpting we dug from the proprietor's formidable stack of timeworn leatherwork magazines. He also informed us that the one and only time he created a leather mask he used ammonia to set it. My friend wanted to purchase ammonia but I was hesitant. I told her that ammonia seemed hazardous and that my way seemed much more innocuous. Yet, in the spirit of investigation, I again agreed to follow her lead.

As I had suspected, the ammonia turned out to be a disastrous idea. One whiff from the bottle had my friend reeling with the effects of toxicity including a headache and light-headedness. We had already cut the basic shapes of our masks from the leather but due to the ammonia incident we had to postpone forming them until the following morning, which was the day of my departure. I had mentioned the need for a face form to shape the leather on, but my friend was insistent that we form the masks on our own faces. Again, it did not seem like a good idea based on my experience with making leather masks. Yet my friend was so enthusiastic about the idea that I again acquiesced.

We each took turns holding the wet gluey leather on the other's face while simultaneously blasting very hot air onto the leather to help form and dry it. I had no idea how awkward and physically uncomfortable the experience would be. In the end my friend agreed that my original suggestions on how to create leather masks really did seem to make the most sense. I thought, "All this silliness to end up right where I would have started in the first place!" Despite the Tricksterish setbacks, we both successfully created thought-provoking masks.

Plumbing Mysteries with Masks

This is an example of approaching the mask making process in reverse – that is, starting with the creation of a mask without having an idea beforehand about the symbols or archetypes contained within and represented by it. This I liken to free drawing, which begins with simply making a mark on a page, followed by another mark, and then seeing where the process leads you. This is a great approach when something unidentified is stirring in the unconscious, as was the case for me. I knew a third mask would be coming, but I had no idea what form it would take. I did not know what symbols or archetypes I would be working with. I was in the depths of a mystery and I created the mask hoping that the archetypes and symbols would reveal themselves and become concretized through the mask so that I could begin consciously working with them.

As is often the case, I was surprised with the mask I had created. When I was cutting the leather I was imagining a Harlequin type of character. After the mask was formed and shaped on my face it looked more like a horned creature than a jester. As we placed our masks together on her sofa to take photos of them, my friend said something about them both representing Dionysus: her mask related to Dionysus on the sea; mine related to Dionysus the horned one. I left her house with my psyche spellbound by Dionysus, the god of masks who has been winking at me from the periphery since the beginning of this project. Now, it seems, he was ready to move out of the shadows and onto center stage in my inner psychic drama.

Figure 15: Horned One Mask

Approaching with Caution

After creating Mask Three it took a while for me to do a ritual to meet the archetypal force it represents. As with the Void mask, I found the new mask intense and intimidating. The level of discomfort I felt in simply viewing the mask indicated that it too is a container for deeply buried unconscious material. Sometimes we have to approach areas of psyche, especially the primal, instinctual parts, with great caution. Like with a wild animal, it can be safest to observe from a distance. It's not always a good idea to rush forward and confront it head on, as this can appear confrontational to these wilder parts of psyche and we run the risk of getting our heads bitten off.

I returned from my trip to the Central Coast and dropped further into the descent, plunged deeper into the *nigredo* phase of the transformation cycle. While on the trip I had shared pieces of my personal story which triggered shame and, in so doing, activated shadow material which had built up around my core wounds. In the weeks following the creation of Mask Three, my psyche was transfixed on the duality of natural forces such as the predator-prey dynamic and the idea of the victim, the sacrifice, and the scapegoat.

Dionysus in the Shadows

I needed to release the tension that was building and direct my attention somewhere constructive, so I began reading about Dionysian initiation for women. While visiting the Central Coast, my friend had recommended I dig deeper into the topic, suggesting that I may find that it has relevance to my work with masks. This study, coupled with a renewed focus on the idea of masks as tools for initiation, provided a revivified sense that a deep and mysterious process was being contained and guided forward by the mask work itself. This re-anchored me in the work. It became even more clear that Dionysus was indeed central to the entire project, including this final mask, though I did not yet understand the intricacy of the patterns being illustrated and illuminated by the masks.

Moving Beyond Reluctance

I found myself reluctant to work with the newly created mask, just as I had been with the Void mask. The way the mask had so strikingly transformed from my simple intention into an unexpected and once again intense symbol evoked uncertainty and mild fear. From its inception, the horned mask had an immediate and powerful presence. The very sight of it affected me. I felt uncomfortable in its presence while also feeling intrigued and incredibly curious about it. The being, archetype, or psychic reality the mask had captured and was trying to convey, seemed quite foreign to me. This mask was truly other. Eventually, I reached a point in the process where I knew I had to nudge myself to approach the mask and embody it in a ritual setting. I put it off for many weeks and too much delay can syphon energy away from these vital psychic stirrings and they can retreat all the way back into the unconscious.

Meanwhile my attention had been captivated by the idea of women's Dionysian initiation. I was studying the ancient Greco-Roman women's initiation mysteries as depicted in a series of murals painted in the Villa of Mysteries in Pompeii, Italy.[3] The initiation story portrayed in the frescoes centers around the myth of Ariadne and Dionysus. The mask of Dionysus appears in the fresco series as a part of the initiatory process, which greatly intrigued me. As I studied and attempted to unravel the esoteric process captured in the murals, the impulse to embody the horned mask took hold and pushed me forward into the following ritual.

Ritual – Meeting the Horned One

I created the ritual conditions in a manner akin to the rituals previously described. This time, I decided not to record it. I had an intuitive hunch to experience the ritual in a state of complete immersion, without concerning myself so much with the role of observer. I performed a ritual cleansing by burning sage and placing a long-forgotten art object on the altar, (which I suddenly remembered and felt compelled to bring in to the ritual). When the ritual space was prepared, I closed my eyes and called in the spirit of the horned mask. I invited the mask spirit to communicate with me. I put the mask on, drew several deep breaths and dropped in, as explained in

Chapter Seven. I began tracking the now familiar shift in my awareness that occurs when the mysterious other of the mask arrives.

With my eyes still closed, I began swaying my head back and forth, from side to side. Within my inner vision I saw a horned beast. It was the image of a bull reflected in a dark mirrored surface. With eyes closed I slowly moved in front of an actual mirror in the room. I opened my eyes and gazed into the mirror. I saw my face masked by the horned visage. My head continued swaying back and forth. When I gazed at myself in the mirror I saw myself and the other being, the spirit of the mask, coexisting together. I experienced this other being as fully present with me. I saw it even when I looked into my own eyes, which was a particularly strange experience. It is impossible to accurately convey the experience in words, similar to how the retelling of a dream does nothing to capture the essence of the dream as experienced by the dreamer.

Embodying the Mysterious Other

The being I encountered was quite different from the presences I experienced with the Star and the Void masks. Rather than appearing as an abstract force guiding me into another realm, this being appeared to merge seamlessly into my waking reality. My ritual with the Horned One mask created an entirely new psychic experience whereby the imaginal realm was meshed with, superimposed upon, and simultaneously coexistent with my ordinary reality. The actual and the imaginal appeared simultaneously in my field of vision. It was literally like experiencing a waking dream.

My embodied experience with the horned mask brought forward and solidified the theme of ambiguity that runs through my earlier masking experiences. I could literally feel within my psyche the presence of an ambiguous force, a force that transcends the notions of good and evil, a force that holds the tension of the opposites in perfect balance. It was like a pure and natural instinct, an unadulterated force of nature. I felt peaceful and solidly grounded in my body. There was no fear, no uncertainty, no questions, and no need to dialogue with the spirit of the mask. I was content to simply let it be present with me. The Horned One mask did not speak to me, as the Star and Void had. It communicated through its presence, its essence, and the physical movements and visions that emerged during the ritual.

Incarnating the Instincts

While wearing the mask, I connected with characteristics and desires which seemed to be unique to the mask. I experienced the spirit behind the Horned One mask as being intrinsically linked to the world of nature. I felt as if I was embodying a pure instinctual force of nature, which is difficult to adequately describe. I felt a deep longing to be out running in a forest, like a wild animal. In my field of vision, a forest of trees appeared, superimposed on the walls that surrounded me. I had a long, involved, and deeply transformative experience in this first ritual with the Horned One mask. It was a crossing over of worlds that has continued to mystify and intrigue me.

Intersecting Worlds

Following is a journal excerpt written immediately after the ritual. It describes the meeting of the imaginal and material realms in a mysterious third space where an initiation story played itself out in this realm between realms. The symbols that appeared in the ritual space correspond with certain stages of the Dionysian women's initiation mysteries depicted in the Villa of Mysteries. This will be explained further in the coming chapters. For now, I invite you to join me in the ritual space and to enter into my active imagination with the Horned One mask.

There is something open, undefended and natural about the spirit that arrived. It is at one with nature – within and without. There is no conflict, no thought, no feeling, only expansive presence. I see it in a wooded area, outside, in nature. I wish to be outside in nature. *The mask spirit wishes to be out in nature*, to move freely in the woods. The presence likes the steady recorded drum beat. It compels me to move in rhythmic steps, walking, almost strutting, like a hoofed beast. My legs feel unusually strong and sturdy, but also light at the same time... There is a sense of absolute peacefulness, groundedness, a sense of seamless connection to all. There is no fear, no questions, no need to dialogue with the spirit. I am content simply allowing it to be present with me, letting it communicate through its presence and the movements.

I am carrying the prayer stick I made at Judith's over a decade ago, the bone wrapped in words, fabric, and sacred symbols (see Appendix C). As I hold the object, I suddenly think of a phallus. I hear a voice, the voice of the mask spirit perhaps, say that it *is* the phallus (masculine principle) which needs to be redeemed and made sacred. I think of the Villa of Mysteries, particularly the part when the woman runs out of the frame of the frescoes and goes to a hidden place underground where the heart of the transformation mysteries are revealed to her. She receives the phallus. In the Villa, this stage of initiatory descent brings the woman face to face with raw animal instincts and with the ambiguous qualities of Nature. In the mural series the initiate instinctively realizes the possibility and danger of identification with the potent archetypal energies, so she goes running out of the painting. She goes somewhere unseen and comes back with the sacred masculine, portrayed as a veiled phallus, in her basket. She is not to look at it directly. She is not to lift the veil or she will perish. Looking at the sacred masculine directly implies identifying with it and claiming it as one's own possession. In the moment, I realize that it is this phase of the mystery rites which is appearing, in real time, in my ritual with the Horned One mask.

Something inside me says that this *is* that mystery. I am with the Horned One, receiving the sacred phallus. As I realize this, my belly literally starts to swell. My abdomen distends with great discomfort, filling like a balloon. I look down and my belly is pushed out as it was in pregnancy. My muscles and tendons feel like they did when I was pregnant. A peculiar physical body memory is activated and my belly literally grows huge and exceedingly uncomfortable. I suddenly think of the pregnant void being filled. I think of the phallus as representing the animating force, the proverbial spark of life that impregnates the empty void and brings forth all life. In that moment, a ceramic spiral falls out of the sacred art object I am still holding. I bend, pick it up off the floor, and tuck it back into the fold of ruby red velvet from which it came.

I hear more words coming from the inner voice. The voice says something about the mother who sacrifices herself to birth the child. I hear: "The mother dies but the child lives. Are you ready to die for your child?" I feel entirely perplexed at these words that are arising. Sophia pops into my mind. I think of how, in her myth, she is said to create on her own, without her male consort. The act of self-creation proves to be a disaster. (Sophia's offspring turns out to be the embodiment of annihilating forces). I think; "What if the baby is a complete abomination, like Ialdoboeth? Is it good to sacrifice oneself for a baby who would grow to cause ultimate destruction and deep suffering?" I think also of Semele, Dionysus' mother and how her life is sacrificed before Dionysus is born. The moment I think this, my belly starts deflating and flattens back to its normal size.

I am stunned by what is occurring in my mind and my physical body. It is truly an active imagination with a force or spirit that has its own life and its own will that is directly affecting my *physical body*. I realize that [after what has happened,] I was expecting the active imagination to lead to a birth. I think: "What's happening? Where's the birth?" I am still walking and walking with an animal's stride. My eyes are open, I see my room, yet I also see the imaginal realm present in the same space. I see blood and what looks like intestines and organs trailing out of me, flowing onto the ground. So much bloody mass.

I realize there will be no birth. I have aborted whatever was filling my womb-space. Then I hear the voice say "Gather it up, gather it up. This is not done. This is not finished." So I retrace my steps. I reach down and collect the imaginal mass into a large ball, much larger than what would have fit inside of my body. I lift it and set it onto what is my bed in the outer world. In the imaginal realm, it is an ancient stone altar. I look up and I see that am at the foot of the Venus of Willendorf, carved out of a great canyon wall, as I drew her over 10 years ago (see Appendix D). Blood is gushing from her vulvic opening. Blood pours out over the stone cliffs and altar, flooding the land. Blood is flowing, flowing, flowing.

I look at the fleshy mass on the altar and see some hints of differentiation beginning to occur. I notice tiny fetuses among the bloody tissue. It looks like some fetuses may be growing. I start trying to push the active imagination in this direction, trying to see new life growing from the mass. Instead, the blood flowing from the Venus turns to water. Water pours and pours, flooding the space I occupy. I am up to my knees in water. It rises higher, flooding the altar, washing up the fetuses and tissue. The water continues flooding until the whole canyon is submerged. I feel as if I am underwater with the mask on. I am scared. (I have had a lifelong fear of drowning, despite the fact that I am a strong swimmer). I want the active imagination to end, but it doesn't. I can move and breathe under the water, but I am frightened nonetheless. I think, "I've had enough, I don't want to drown in this. I am afraid of drowning in the deep unconscious waters." At this realization, the water begins to recede and drain away.

Now the rocky canyon walls have verdant growth spouting from them. The Venus is covered with lush, mossy life. On the altar there is a deep leafy green bundle. I approach it and petal after petal of green leaves begin peeling back. In the center of the bundle there is a tiny baby made of light substance. The infant is glowing. I want to pick it up, but am hesitant. I'm not sure if it's okay for me to touch it. I'm not sure if I'm supposed to or not. The voice says, "Hurry up! Pick it up! This is your baby." I pick it up and hold it in front of me to examine its little body. It's a tiny glowing human. I notice that it's a hermaphrodite - it has both male and female sex organs. I think, "Wow, I just birthed a baby hermaphrodite?" And just then it sprouts wings. I am holding a winged baby hermaphrodite. I press it against my body, holding it to my chest and it absorbs into me. *I* begin to sprout wings. I am still wearing the horned mask, so I become a horned one with wings. I again tune into the presence of the animal, the instinctual one. I begin walking again, but the imaginal wings are heavy, literally making it difficult for me to move my body. I feel lightheaded. I feel an impulse to lay on my bed in the yogic child's pose. The wings fold in around me, protecting me and creating a cocoon. I close my eyes and just rest, motionless.

As I lie there I see in my mind's eye a white glowing stone, similar to one that came into my psyche on a wilderness vision quest undertaken during the this masking project. I immediately remember a pair of actual crystals that a relative gave me many years ago. It occurs to me that they are a physical, external embodiment of the internal stone symbol that continues to appear in dreams, active imaginations, and on the vision quest. I hear the voice say "The stones were passed to you. These are sacred stones of power. They hold the power of the Wounded healer. This is your inheritance. It was too heavy a burden for [my relative], so the stones were passed on to you. [This relative] was the chosen healer, the shaman of [their] generation, but there was no container, no guides. The tests and trials broke [the relative], split [them]. The stones were passed to you. The ancestors chose you." Then I heard something like: "With great power comes great responsibility." I giggle, thinking of the Spider Man movie.

I suddenly feel the real spider bites that I woke up with a few days earlier. They're on my left ankle, the ankle I shattered and which left me incapacitated for nearly a year – a year of profound spiritual initiation. In the moment I think of the swollen, irritated bites as sacred spider bites, as the sacred venom, the healing poison. I hear a line from a poem I wrote over twenty years ago, "I drink the poison so I can be pure." I think to myself, as I lay on my bed with the Horned One mask still covering my face: "I took in the poison, the ancestral poison, in order to transmute it. The poison festered inside of me and forced me into a cleansing, a purification. In cleansing out the family poison I also began cleansing out my own poison - on a deep soul, perhaps even karmic, level." My thoughts continue: "The poisoning led to the cleansing which then caused a much deeper cleansing, beyond removing the passed on poison, to removing the deep seated, karmic poison." (It was something like this. It is hard to put words to. It came to me as a knowing, not as words).

The dizziness and light-headed feeling passes. I stand, holding the imaginal stone. I begin walking again, this time with the imaginal stone. I am holding it securely, holding it as sacred. I hear the voice say there is no more need for words, no need for questions, that all is being revealed through the vision itself. I am assured that there will be time for talking later, if I still find it necessary. I lie back down on the bed and hold the stone to my solar plexus. The stone absorbs into my body. I feel the spirit of the mask leave me, right then. I know the ritual and active imagination is complete. I take the mask off and return to an ordinary state of consciousness. (Azaria, personal journal entry, July 14, 2012).

There are far too many themes and symbols presented in this first ritual with the Horned One mask to examine herein. For the sake of brevity and clarity, I have chosen to review only a select few symbols that arose during the ritual and focus on those that are most significant to the scope of this book. I will amplify the chosen symbols in the next chapter and then survey the over-arching themes that arose in the ritual. After that I will apply them to my personal process, so you can see how this all fits together.

TINA AZARIA

End Notes

1. Nor Hall, 1988, p.198
2. Nichols, 1980
3. Fierz-David, 1980

18 CONSCIOUS APPROACH

Amplifying the Archetypes and Symbols

The Bull

The first symbol that appeared in association with the horned mask was the bull, a symbol of masculine strength and power.[1] The bull represents pure animalistic instincts and fecund creative powers, as well as the potency found when nature is harnessed in service of humankind. The domestication of the bull was pivotal to our ability to create civilizations centered on agriculture. Forceful, strong, and untiring, the bull was used to plow the earth and harvest crops to the extent that stable communities became possible.[2] The bull was revered for its drive and energy. The sexual fertility of the bull coupled with its nearly inexhaustible power is likely the root of the bull's designation as a sacred masculine being.

The bull represents the pure life force energy underlying and animating the natural world.[3] In ancient times the bull was associated with the sky, the sun, and the moon. As a tremendous power of nature, the bull was believed to be connected to all four elements – earth, air, fire and water. Yet, the bull's connection with the element of water was perhaps one of its most venerated associations. In ancient Egypt and Mesopotamia, the bull was considered to be the force behind the annual flooding of the life-giving rivers (the Nile and the Tigris, respectively). The words for bull and rain in Sanskrit are derived from the same root, signifying both "to water" and "to impregnate."[4]

Fertile Creativity

The bull appears as an important part of mythological traditions around the world.[5] In Eastern mythology, the Indian god Shiva is accompanied by his bull, Nandi, who is connected to Shiva's reproductive powers and is associated with the sacred phallus. Nandi, a symbol of fertility, embodies both the powers of destruction and generative creativity.[6]

The bull not only represents the traditionally masculine symbols of the sun and the phallus, but also holds associations with the Feminine principle. The shape of the bull's horns has been connected with the moon, a traditionally feminine symbol in the West, as well as with the uterus and fallopian tubes. In this way, the bull signifies the balance of forces that underlie fertility and creativity.[7]

Dionysus the Bull God

In Greece, Dionysus, god of the mask, was also worshipped as the bull god. During festivals honoring the bull, giant phalluses were carried in processions honoring Dionysian sexual exuberance. One of Dionysus' many monikers was "the horned deity."[8] It was in his bull form, as Dionysus Zagreus, that he was dismembered by the Titans and then later resurrected after his heart was saved.[9] Psychologically, the symbol of the bull speaks to our relationship to instinctual nature. It represents the confrontation between the unbridled virility of bull-like animal impulses and notions of civilized social norms. The deep psychic energy of the raging bull can appear threatening to the controlled persona and is often so well-hidden that when it shows up in dreams or active imaginations, it can seem entirely "other."[10] The bull points to creative fertility, not only physically, but on all dimensions of being. It is connected to the idea of extreme productivity.

When the bull appeared in the active imagination, I experienced such a complete union with it that it did not feel threatening or foreign to me. To the contrary, the presence of the bull felt completely natural, comfortable, and in some hard to explain way, equalizing. In that moment with the bull I felt a physical, emotional, and psychological equilibrium like I never have before. This experience with the horned mask has had a long-term impact on my psyche, which I further describe in the coming chapters. The arrival of the bull in conjunction with the horned mask was a clear indication to me that Dionysus, god of both bull and mask, was a central archetype being evoked from my work with masks. Dionysus had moved out from the shadows to take center stage in my work with masks.

The Villa of Mysteries

Symbols of ancient women's initiation rites arose early in the ritual with the Horned One mask. During the time when I was deeply involved in ritual work with the mask (but months after I had created the mask), I was simultaneously studying women's mystery rites, particularly those depicted in the Italian Villa of Mysteries. In 1909, a series of frescoes was unearthed in this famous villa that lies on the outskirts of the ancient city of Pompeii.[11] The murals in the Villa of Mysteries depict women engaged in a cycle of activities that are believed to explain the process of initiation into the mysteries of the cult of Dionysus (also known as the Orphic mysteries). The mystery rites illustrated appear to portray initiatory preparations preceding a marriage.[12] It is believed by some that the images provide an account of the stages of subjective development (similar to individuation) undergone by ancient women.[13] See Appendix E for images of the Villa Frescoes.

Materially Present Myths

The mythic narrative illustrated in the central mystery chamber of the villa, the Initiation Hall, has been examined from several perspectives, including that of depth psychology.[14] In the early 1950s at the Jung Institute in Zurich, Docent Linda Fierz-David presented a series of lectures on women's Dionysian initiation, based on the frescoes. In her presentations she examined the images in terms of their relationship to the process of individuation. She described the designs as outwardly simple yet obviously portraying a sequence of actions that together form a complex, coherent event. Some of the figures appear to be contemporary portraits. Others are clearly mythological beings portrayed as being *materially present* with the women pictured as performing initiation rites in the hall. The phenomenon of mythic figures being physically present with real-life initiates is an intriguing concept, one that seems to mirror the experience I had in the ritual with the Horned One mask.

The main mythic figures in the initiation frescoes include the god Dionysus and his bride Ariadne. In the introduction to a book comprised of Fierz-David's lectures, M. Esther Harding[15] expresses the meaning behind the intentional depiction of the mysterious overlap between mundane and mythic time in the following quote:

> The reality of the main figures makes it clear that the series is not merely the representation of a myth, but is rather, intended to portray the inner psychological experience in which the background material and drama which are usually entirely unconscious are activated. We ordinarily experience such things in dreams, but under certain circumstances, the "stuff as dreams are made on" appears before the inner eye as if it were objectively real and really happening. Such experiences do have an emotional reality, and they can affect the individuals profoundly, perhaps causing a deep and permanent transformation of their personality.

Beyond the Bounds of Psyche

The above quote captures the essence of the experience I had in the ritual of the imaginal realm appearing as objectively real. Months after my ritual encounter with the Horned One, I read a book by Jeffrey Raff, *The Wedding of Sophia,*[16] which offered the clearest explanation I have found so far on the phenomena experienced in the ritual. In summary, Raff differentiates between experiences that occur strictly within the bounds of the individual psyche and those imaginal experiences that bleed over into the external environment and appear to occur in a space beyond the human psyche. I believe Raff's theories, which I explore in greater detail in Chapter Twenty One, may help to explain my experience of the imaginal realm appearing as *materially present* and the significant and mysterious transformations brought about by this occurrence.

Dionysian and Orphic Initiation Mysteries

Initiation into the cult of Dionysus centralized around the mysterious union of the educated, civilized woman with the powerful instinctual forces represented by Dionysus in his many varied forms.[17] In modern society, as in ancient times, there exists a psychological need to integrate the unconscious forces embodied in the symbol of the bull. The qualities the bull embodies parallel what Jung referred to as primitive instincts, such as sexual desire and aggression.[18]

Archetypes and Instincts

For our purposes here it is important to note that archetypes are intrinsically linked with, but not identical to instincts.[19] According to Jung, instincts are embedded in the physical body and enter the psyche as impulses, thoughts, and emotions.[20] Humans, like other animals, are influenced by physiological processes and needs that move from soma to psyche. For example, hunger and sexuality are instinctual drives based in the body. While they may influence us, they do not ultimately determine our behavior – we can choose when and how to satisfy our physical drives. Archetypes, on the other hand, enter the psyche from the mental plane, as images and symbols.

Psyche's Spectrum

Jung uses the metaphor of the spectrum of light to illustrate his concept of the spectrum of psyche.[21] In this model, instincts lie at the lower, infrared end of the spectrum and archetypes lie at the higher, ultraviolet end. This means that we are motivated by instincts on one end of the spectrum of psyche, and by mental images and symbols on the other end. Jung believed that instincts relinquish control of the psyche at a certain point on the spectrum when the instinctive impulse reaches what he refers to as a spiritual form, a higher form represented by symbols and archetypes. Although related to instincts, the archetypes transcend biological determinism and are connected more with the human mind and spirit than with the body.[22]

Respecting Nature's Forces

In the mystery cults of old, the powerful force of primitive, animalistic instincts were approached with reverence and great humility so that the experience would not be destructive or chaotic. By respecting the power of the instinctive nature and holding a sacred attitude toward it, the ancient initiate experienced a mysterious union with the ambivalent instinctive forces which led to a complete renewal of life energy.[23] In the following quote from the introduction the Fierz-David's book, Harding[24] emphasizes the importance of approaching the instinctual forces free of the hubris of the ego:

> Union with primitive instinctual forces, represented in the [Villa frescoes] series in symbolic form as a phallic god, cannot be sought for personal satisfaction or aggrandizement without serious consequences. These forces must be approached with a deep religious spirit. The recognition that the ego is only part of the total personality, and not even the most important part, is essential if the experience is to lead to life and not to death.

Holding an attitude of reverence was considered a matter of life and death in terms of the successful initiation of the individual psyche into the mysteries of Dionysus. If approached correctly, there is a unification of spiritual life with mundane reality. Ordinary life becomes infused with divine meaning and the world of matter is en-souled. On the other hand, an improper, hasty, or arrogant approach could just as easily lead to the death of the individual personality at the hands of the primitive instincts.[25] This idea is comparable to the concept of possession by an archetype, whereby an archetype-centered complex takes over the personality so completely that the individualized consciousness all but disappears.[26]

In contemporary society, dogmatic religious and moral structures discourage and inhibit individualized expression of the human soul. There is a push-pull dynamic between doing what the ego and persona deem to be acceptable and following instinctual impulses that well up from the individual and collective unconscious. It is a natural reaction to turn towards the instinctual depths when confronted with the rigid dogmatization of culture and religion. However, instead of approaching the deeper instincts with a conscious, serious attitude, as was held in the past, the modern plunge into the instinctual depths is often comparable to a self-serving orgy which can be wildly destructive.[27]

This is the notorious plunge into the realms of uninhibited sex, indulgence in mind-altering drugs, and ecstatic states brought on by hypnotic music, as was introduced in the 1960s and has been carried through into contemporary expressions such as raves and festivals. Entering into states of ecstatic self-abandon are often associated with Dionysus as god of wine, music, ecstasy and, of course, the trance-inducing mask. Instead of enhancing life, an unconscious dance with instinctual nature dissipates the deep psychic life force represented by the bull.

According to Fierz-David[28], the narrative presented in the initiation hall of the Villa of Mysteries seems to warn that "arrogance or self-seeking may lead to a disastrous inflation, portrayed as if it were a regular hazard on the initiation path." This warning is echoed in Jung and von Franz's observations that when the gods are approached, in other words, when the Self archetype is constellated, inflation often occurs.

I am reminded of the warnings against inflation that I encountered in reading about the Star as a symbol of the Self. Jung frequently associated the Self with the archetype of God, as an image of totality and undivided wholeness. He warned that the numinous Self should always be approached with an air of humility and a certain distance, lest one become identified with the archetype and then become inflated.[29] The Self, just as many god figures, is represented as an ambiguous and powerful archetype capable of both creation and destruction - which is perhaps why the theme of punishment for hubris is so pervasive in world mythology.[30]

End Notes

1. Ronnberg & Martin, 2010
2. Ronnberg & Martin, 2010
3. Kerenyi, 1976
4. Ronnberg & Martin, 2010)
5. Wilkinson, 2009
6. Ronnberg & Martin, 2010
7. Gimbutas, 1991
8. Kerenyi, 1976
9. Kerenyi, 1976
10. Ronnberg & Martin, 2010
11. Gazda, 2000
12. Gazda, 2000
13. Fierz-David, 1980
14. Fierz-David, 1980; Hall, 1988
15. Fierz-David, 1980, p. xi
16. Raff, 2003
17. Fierz-David, 1980; Kerenyi, 1976
18. Stein, 1998
19. Robertston, 1987; Stein, 1998; Stevens, 1982
20. Stein, 1998
21. Stein, 1998
22. Stein, 1998
23. Fierz-David, 1980
24. Fierz-David, 1980, p. xiii
25. Fierz-David, 1980
26. Stein, 1998
27. Fierz-David, 1980
28. Fierz-David, 1980, p.20
29. Stein, 1998
30. Wilkinson, 2010

19 OPPOSITES UNITE

The Sacred Marriage

The story of the mystical marriage provides a basic mythic structure, or map, for understanding the ancient initiation process, which parallels the modern experience of individuation. In the ancient Greco-Roman mystery rites an act of redemption occurs through the union of opposites. As we return to the myth of Ariadne and Dionysus, we see that their marriage on the isle of Naxos leads to the redemption of both god and mortal.

The male and female counterparts, combined, serve as a symbol of the Self, the unified whole. Psychologically, they personify both the Self and the *process of becoming* an individualized Self – uniting and holding the opposites in perfect balance.[1] The sacred union between the two opposites (represented as the Feminine and Masculine Principles) is at the heart of the mystery traditions of the Mediterranean region.[2]

The Redeeming Union

In Chapter Fourteen, we left Ariadne at the point in the myth where, having been abandoned by the hero Theseus on the isle of Naxos, she hangs herself in despair, a symbol of the ultimate sacrifice. In the myth, the transformation occurs at the moment of Ariadne's death. At that very instant, Dionysus arrives by way of the sea. The two do not recognize one another at first. Ariadne, expecting death, finds Dionysus; he, searching for his ancient underworld mother, finds Ariadne. Ariadne succumbs to death, but is mysteriously resurrected by Dionysus' life-giving power and his love for her. They immediately wed and in this mysterious, sacred union on the isle of Naxos, both mortal and god are transformed.

Ariadne's life is restored and in this restorative act, Dionysus demonstrates his innate power which in turn elevates his status from half-god (as son of Zeus and the mortal Semele) to a full god, able to dwell on Mount Olympus. Together, the couple ascend to the heavens following their mystical union. To honor Ariadne, Dionysus tosses into the sky a crown of seven stars which he had given Ariadne (which becomes the constellation known as The Seven Sisters). Dionysus becomes Ariadne's redeemer, and both parties are restored to wholeness. The inner workings of the transformative union are left a mystery, one that ancient initiates explored within the frescoed walls of the Villa of Mysteries.

Spirit and Matter Unite

In the initiation rites, an inner union takes place in the psyche of the initiate which mirrors the mystical union of opposites portrayed in the myth. Esther Harding[3] explains the psychological implications of the redeeming union for the human initiate: "She thus experiences the transforming power of union with the dual aspects of intense life – the ecstatic, life-giving spirit and the ecstasy of immersion in the instinctive stream of life that underlies and precedes conscious self-determination." The inner union is centered on reconciling the tension between the lower, instinctual self – the animal body that craves, devours, and suffers and the higher, spiritual nature of human beings.

The sacred union is a metaphor for the union of spirit with matter, the mysterious act that makes matter holy once again by elevating it to the spiritual level and thereby redeeming it. I cannot help but be reminded of the idea that masks are material objects that become enlivened by a spirit when they are worn – literally spirit uniting with matter. Perhaps it is this very concept that has earned masks the designation of sacred objects in many cultures.

Alchemical Coniunctio

I will quickly review the alchemical process of transformation, culminating in the union of opposites, the *coniunctio*, which yields the Philosopher's Stone. As a reminder, the image of a magical stone was the final symbol to appear in my first active imagination with the Horned One mask. For Jung[4] the alchemical process is an apt metaphor for the individuation process and the stone, a symbol for the Self Archetype which is the manifestation of a truly unified consciousness.

This magical stone, the goal of the entire alchemical opus, was reputed to transform matter, heal sickness, reveal the mysteries of spirit, and bestow immortality on its creator.[5] The stone begins in an undifferentiated state as a chaotic mixing of the initial substance, known as the *prima materia*.[6] This is the indeterminate state that is there at the beginning of the process. It's the place of internal confusion and chaos that leads us down the path of growth in the first place. The transformation process begins with differentiating the original matter into its constituent parts, which must take place in the *vas hermetica*, the alchemical vessel, or container. The component substances are comprised of various pairs of opposites which must first be separated and then re-united. Jung continually pointed out that psychic opposites tend to arrange themselves in pairs or quaternities.[7] Of this he says:

> [F]irst there is a point. Pairs of opposites emanate out of that point, left and right, above and below, inner and outer. Then, to the extent that those emanated opposites lose connection with their source, they are at war with each other...And only to the extent that they can reconnect with their source are they then mediated and reconciled. The central point, which is both their source on the one hand and their reconciling mediator on the other, is *Mercurius*.[8]

The Transforming Trickster Guide

As mentioned earlier in this book, *Mercurius*, both Trickster and guide, is a transformative agent that has the ability to change shapes and cross between realms.[9] Jung believed this spirit of shape-shifting, this ambiguous Trickster force, is at the heart of transformation. This, of course, makes sense when one considers the fact that in order to transform, the being or object involved must, by necessity, be able to change its shape or form. In terms of my work, the masks served as the means by which I was able to shape-shift and change not only my external appearance, but also my inner psychic state.

The Heights and Depths

In his very last book, a heady tome on the mysterious union of opposites, *Mysterium Coniunctionis*, Jung[10] describes the opposites as represented by the symbols of the sun and moon, or *sol* and *luna* in alchemy, which are considered masculine and feminine forces, respectively. He suggests that the mind turns upward toward the spirit of god, and this aspect shines like the sun. There is also a part of the human mind that turns toward the "waters under the firmament," toward sense-based experience. Jung[11] says: "In both cases it is clearly the human spirit or psyche, both of which have, however, a double aspect, one facing upwards to the light, the other downwards to the darkness ruled by the moon." In other words, a part of us is turned toward the world of consciousness and seeks transcendent experiences of the divine. Another part of us is naturally turned inward toward the depths of the unconscious and the instinctual depths. The latter part longs for immanent experiences which can be described as experiences of the divine spark within.

There is a longing, often repressed, to have direct contact with *Zoe*, the animating life force as it manifests here and now in the material world. Jung believed we must unify these opposing tendencies if we are to have internal harmony. In ancient Crete, this concept is alluded to in the myth of Ariadne's union with Dionysus. In alchemy, the opposites are symbolized as the King and Queen.

Mystical Union

After many rounds of separation and purification are complete, the final, most distinguished (distilled) pair of opposites, represented as the King and the Queen, is then united in the *coniunctio,* the mystical marriage. From this union of opposites the Philosopher's Stone emerges. This is described, in depth psychological terms, as the *transcendent function* - the union of opposing forces within the psyche which leads to a new state of consciousness.[12]

From the one undifferentiated original state comes the two, in the form of the opposites. When the two are adequately separated and purified they can be then united to bring forth a new unified whole, which has become increasingly refined and potent from the *coniunctio.* In reality, the process of individuation, like alchemy, never ends. The Philosopher's Stone of the previous process becomes the *prima materia* of the next. Each consecutive stage reveals a more purified and powerful version of the stone.[13] The cycle of transformation continues, as far as we know, until death.

Symbols of Balance

From the very beginning, the spirit of the Horned One mask seemed to hold the opposites in a natural and uncontrived balance. In the visionary imaginal experience that accompanied the ritual, symbols of the masculine and feminine clearly came forward as the phallus and the pregnant void, as well as in the symbols of the bull and the Venus. The image of the union of opposite appeared as the symbol of pregnancy and particularly in the symbol of the *hermaphrodite,* a being that is simultaneously female and male.[14]

Veiled in Mystery

In retrospect, I was able to see that the concepts presented in Jung's *Mysterium Coniunctionis,* the ideas surrounding the mysterious union of psychic opposites, were present in the active imagination with the Horned One mask. This type of experience follows the esoteric women's mystery traditions of ancient Mediterranean cultures, as depicted in the myth of Dionysus and Ariadne. It is important to note that in these ancient rites, the key initiatory experience remains veiled and obscured even to the initiate. It is only the symbols surrounding the transformation, and the accompanying results of the mystery rite, that are fully illuminated.[15]

The process of alchemical transformation of the soul is exemplified in the myths of Dionysus and Ariadne. In the myth Ariadne undergoes a separation from her previous state. She falls into chaos and confusion until she finally surrenders in an act of self-sacrifice, to death. The process of redemption occurs through union with her divine counterpart, her masculine opposite. The transformation that occurs as a result of the sacred marriage, which is referred to as *redemption,* is the crux of the mystery rites surrounding their myths.

The Mystery of Redemption

By standard definition, the word redeem means to release from blame or debt; to rescue or retrieve; to make good or atone; and to free from captivity, distress, or harm.[16] The idea of redemption, as it appears in the myth, is based on the idea of falling from an original state of wholeness into the darkness of self-alienation, followed by an act of complete surrender. It is the act of surrender that leads to death. The release of the old form brings about a sacred union where the opposites harmonize. The union brings on the redemption which symbolizes restoration to a state of wholeness and balance.

A depth psychological understanding of redemption differs from the Christian theological perspective on redemption, which is a concept with many connotations beyond what is discussed herein. In many myths, the idea of redemption refers to a condition in which a person has been magically downcast, or cursed, so that they engage in behavior that is fundamentally destructive.[17] In the myth examined, Ariadne becomes spellbound by external forces, represented by Theseus, the hero. The bewitchment causes her to abandon her true nature, her origin. In a bewitched state, she is lured away from her true self and falls into a state of complete darkness represented by deep sleep, followed by death.

Dionysian Liberation

Ariadne is portrayed as undergoing the process of redemption through her union with Dionysus, who represents the redeeming principle. Dionysus, although thoroughly masculine, was known throughout antiquity as a god who related directly to women, and to the Great Mother herself. In psychological terms, Dionysus represents the masculine spark of life in the psyches of all women. In his book *Return of the Goddess,* author Edward Whitmont[18] describes the role of the Dionysian principle in women's psychological development. He says, "As Dionysus returns, the repression of the feminine can no longer continue." In other words, Dionysus was reputed to have a liberating effect on the feminine psyche. His myths are instructive in this regard.

Arriving from the outskirts of civilization, Dionysus would sweep though villages and enchant domestically enslaved women away from their life of never-ending mundane tasks. In his role as liberator of women, he would call them out into the woods and wild places where they would dance ecstatically under the moonlight, intoxicated by wine and the frenzied beat of primal drums. He pushed these otherwise controlled matrons into wild ecstatic states, freeing them from the chains of their social roles and domestic duties and liberating them from identification with their pasts.[19]

Dionysus as Redeemer

Dionysus is a liberating principle that releases everything that has been locked up and repressed[20]. His arrival is known to induce immense joy and terror at the same time. With Dionysus, redemption occurs through the release of buried emotions, repressed instinctual desires, and a rush of inspired creative expression that can be experienced as pure ecstasy. Author Helen Deutsch[21] describes the act of surrender and the accompanying freedom from duality experienced by followers of Dionysus:

> In the state of ecstasy that was the mark of his follower, the spirit of god was believed to enter the human being and take possession of [her] in a kind of mystic community. The belief of his worshipers was that, in such a union with god, they too were immortal. The emotional experience of the unification of another being with him, as the god, was his proof of achieved divinity. He was a mad, raving, god, but he was at the same time a giver of enchanting joy and peace. There was no more man-woman, hate-love:

there was an end to the struggle of polarities. He was then known as the god of freedom.

Dionysian energy is potent and carries with it paradoxical experiences and the potential for deep transformation that comes from embracing ambiguity. Dionysus unites humankind with nature and frees the feminine principle from the confines of civilized roles, bringing women back to their own instinctual depths.

The Return of Ambiguity

In the ritual with the Horned One mask, the theme of ambiguity arose immediately. The force or presence that arrived though the horned mask was the embodiment of ambiguity – being neither light nor dark, neither good nor bad. Perhaps the ambiguous, instinctual force I experienced was akin to the Dionysian principle. As I mentioned in Chapter Three, ambivalence is said to be central to the art of masking, and to Dionysus, god of the mask.[22] For some reason, even though I had read about the connection between masking and ambiguity, I was still surprised when my *embodied experience* with the Horned One mask was one of absolute ambiguous life force.

The ambiguity I have experienced in masking is apparently quite common. It stands to reason that masks are often used in indigenous cultures to invoke the gods, and the gods are very often ambiguous beings. The following quote from Napier[23] helped me to see that my personal experiences do have a connection, however hazy, to the larger human continuum of masking traditions. Napier says: "If we posit a pantheon of such ambivalent figures, as is the case in Greek antiquity, we make an initial step toward recognizing the significance of masks for cultures in which ambivalence is a primary cosmological factor." As I explored the masks I began to wonder: Is my primary cosmological story, my personal creation myth, one of divine, pervasive ambiguity? I did not yet have a definitive answer to this question, but I did feel I was getting closer to it with each ritual. What I did unquestionably gain from my preliminary work with the Horned One mask was a deep, *embodied knowing* of ambiguity itself. I felt it through to my bones.

End Notes

1. Fierz-David, 1980
2. Fierz-David, 1980; Kerenyi, 1976
3. Fierz-David, 1980 p. xii
4. Jung, 1963
5. Raff 2000, 2003; Edinger, 1991, 1995
6. Edinger, 1991
7. Edinger, 1994, p. 22
8. Jung, as quoted in Edinger, 1994, p. 32
9. Raff, 2000
10. Jung, 1963
11. Jung, 1963, p.143
12. Edinger, 1991, 1995; Swartz-Salant, 1995
13. Edinger, 1995
14. Ronnberg & Martin, 2010
15. Fierz-David, 1980; Hall, 1988
16. Merriam-Webster, 1973
17. von Franz, 1956
18. Whitmont, 1984, p.120
19. Deutsch,1969; Kerenyi, 1976
20. Edinger, 1994
21. Deutsch, 1969, p. 31
22. Napier, 1986; Nunley & McCarty, 1999
23. Napier, 1986 p. xxv

20 SHADOW INTEGRATION

The first phase in initiation is a ritual death. This is the turning away or removal of the initiate from their "ordinary" daily life and placing them in ritual seclusion. The ego surrenders to something unknown and larger – in depth terms, these are the impulses and information coming from the unconscious. The ego must realize it's not in charge, and thus, approach with humility and caution. The initiate must be devoted to the work, otherwise, they may not be able to push through the initiatory ordeal and come out the other side successfully.

Dionysian Initiation Rites

So we can say that the initiation process begins with the offering, the sacrifice. In the case of Dionysian initiation, it is the offering up of oneself to the larger forces of life and death, as Ariadne did on the isle of Naxos. Psychologically, it is the ego surrendering to the fact that it is not in control and, it is a coming to terms of the ego with the realities of heartache and betrayal. It is surrendering the parts of the ego that have been wounded, the parts that have suffered and, consequently, have been enslaved to a life of struggle.

Initiation Masks

The way this translates to my own work with the masks is as follows: I first offered up the uninitiated parts of my ego to the work with as much humility and sincerity as I could find inside myself, knowing fully that there were forces at work that are beyond my ego consciousness. I devoted myself to the work with the masks and subsequently, to the initiation process and the work of individuation. I had to turn away from the "human world" and separate myself from the life I had been living. I then submitted myself wholeheartedly to the slow and painful process of becoming conscious of my own shadow material through working with the masks.

Personal Shadow

As already explained, the next stage following the surrender is descent into the unconscious. First, one goes into the personal unconscious, which is often described as a return to childhood. For me, this material came forward in my work with the Void mask. The foray into the shadow realms of the personal unconscious was, for me, a return to the wounded child and the fear and shame that was held there, quietly siphoning off libido. This stage brought me eye to eye with the places of my own arrested development in terms of my creative expression.

Primitive Psyche

The next stage of initiation brings a deeper descent into shadow and moves one into the realm of the collective unconscious. This phase is a meeting with the primitive, instinctual psyche. This cannot be a mindless plunge into the depths. In order for the process to remain conscious, the mature developed ego must remain present and watchful if the unconscious is going to be integrated into consciousness.

At this point, the conscious mind wrestles to understand what is happening. It does not easily comprehend this phase of psychic initiation. Grappling with the logical mind is simply a part of the process at this stage. I, myself, found the experience with the

Horned One mask to be one that defies logical explanation. I truly believe I encountered the embodiment of the raw power of the instinctual psyche in my very first ritual with the mask. My *experience* was one of profound transformation. Yet I came out of the experience unable to explain it. However, there is no doubt in my mind that the things I *felt* in the ritual were real enough to impart lasting changes in my personality.

Encountering Primal Instincts

The meeting with the masculine numinous (represented by the bull and the phallus in the ritual) is a powerful experience similar to descriptions of maddening Dionysian ecstasy. The initiation stories warn that the initiate may easily become identified with her numinous experience. It is not until she is chastised by a darker force that she feels guilt and dismay from her near-act of sacrilege in thinking that the god-spark within is her personal possession. Only then does she come to her senses and return to a state of modesty or humility. Humility would certainly be violated if any human woman claimed to be, in her own person, the elected bride of the god of instinct, creativity, and inspiration. Such an attitude would inflate a mortal woman; distorting her self-perception and making her feel as if she is above others as the bride of god.[1]

Initiatory Humbling

This phase of initiation is portrayed in the Villa of Mysteries as a dark angel chastising the initiate, and presumably is an important step in the coniunctio. Fortunately, the initiation process itself helps the initiate realize her near mistake. As she becomes conscious of it, she becomes cleansed. It is the act of becoming conscious which purifies her of unwanted influences, especially hubris. After the cleansing, the "atonement," the initiate is no longer over-confident and self-assured. She has been humbled by a collision with the forces of the divine and the unconscious which remind her of her true place, which is neither above nor below others. The initiate comes to realize that she (her ego) is not omnipotent and that her ego consciousness is a lesser force than the archetypal Self. The initiate realizes that although she unites with a divine force, she herself is not divine. This idea harkens back to von Franz[2] saying that the appearance of the Star of Bethlehem signifies that we mortal women are not divine beings, but we are the stable into which divinity is born. This realization cleanses the initiate of hubris. The process humbles her and thereby renders her "born again."

Self-Evident Restoration

After the cleansing the initiate is portrayed in the myths as emerging, purified and restored. In the ancient mystery rites, the initiate would re-emerge in the world and enter into the company of a sisterhood of mature, initiated women whose wisdom was manifest and obvious. They did not need to assert themselves or their value. Their value was apparent. Esther Harding[3] describes these ancient initiated women: "They are among the wise ones, simple, natural, and at one with themselves; whose inner dignity needs no advertisement, it is self-evident."

Uniting with the Inner Opposite

The crux of the initiation is that human woman unites with the masculine creative force *within* and in the union, becomes more whole and balanced. Then, through embracing her transformation with genuine humility, the woman returns to the world as one who is truly wise. This is my interpretation of the transformation-through-union motif portrayed in the myth of Ariadne/Dionysus and mirrored in my personal experience in the ritual with the Horned One mask.

Masks as Guides

It was unquestionably my work with the masks which served to crystalize the symbols that ended up pointing me to ancient initiation myths. The myths then provided a map that helped me to see clearly, and thereby *make conscious*, my own process of psychological initiation as induced and guided by the masks.

While the Guiding Star mask got me in touch with the Self Archetype, my inner divine spark, it also warned me against hubris. The Void mask dropped me into the wounded areas within my personal shadow. In my work with the Horned One mask, both the instinctual psyche and the masculine principle came forward to reveal deeper layers of presence in my own psyche.

At the time, I had not been looking in this direction in my personal healing process. I would not have thought to examine my relationship to the inner masculine had the masks not provoked this. I had already integrated many characteristics of the masculine principle while raising my sons as a single mother. I had stepped into mothering and fathering roles, becoming not only the nurturer but also the sole protector, provider, and disciplinarian. Furthermore, I'd grown up with a mother who had fairly balanced feminine and masculine qualities and so I had this modeled to me my entire life. I have always been fairly balanced in regard to my yin and yang qualities. I think this is the reason I was not focusing on integrating the masculine in my personal work, until I began working with the masks.

Separating the Layers of Psyche

The mask work brought my personal wounds around the masculine to the forefront. This work was not at all new to me. I had already been working with these same psychological and emotional wounds for over twenty years. The difference this time was that the masks crystallized the work for me in an entirely new and powerful way. I experienced true separation of the material in a way that clearly revealed what level of the unconscious I was working with at any given point. Through working with the masks, I was able to separate the personal from the collective and the collective from the archetypal.

With the Void mask I connected with the inner wounds, the inner scapegoat complex, and the concept of sacrifice. With the Horned One mask, I connected with the inner savior, the redeeming spark of life within my own psyche. The mysterious union I experienced in the ritual with the mask led to profound changes in my psyche. I gained a renewed perspective on my life experiences and much of the shame I was carrying was simply gone after doing this work. I have worked to release this shame many times through many different methods, but somehow, mysteriously, the mask work penetrated deeper levels to release shame from my *body*.

Embodied Release

My encounters with the ambiguous forces of nature that are embodied in the masks have shifted my perspective of my life story in relationship to the larger human story. Through this work I experienced something akin to getting over myself, as it were. I am no longer so identified with my story of wounding which I have experienced so much shame around. A healthy distancing is occurring so that I am beginning to come into proper relationship with my own creative work that largely sprung from my core wounds.

I moved into a more solid place of no longer swinging between the poles of being inflated or deflated in relationship to the creative impulses that move through me. Because of this work with the masks, I am no longer over-valuing or undervaluing the creativity that moves through me. Nor am I considering the creative impulses to be my personal possession. I see, even more deeply and truly, that I am merely the stable into which they have been born. My creative work is not mine to keep locked away. It comes from a deeper source and has a life of its own. I have known this in my mind, but now I really *know* this in my body.

Masks and Gnosis

Through the mask work, I have undergone a form of gnosis where I have come to know the divine spark within *experientially*. As a result I finished this project not only ready, but yearning to get my creative work out into the world as soon as possible. Soon after, I published my first book of poetry and art, which I had begun over a decade earlier but had been continually unable to complete. This marked a complete shift in attitude compared to where I was when I began the masking process described in this book.

I learned to completely stop looking outside of myself for "redemption" or "salvation," or even guidance. I even more consciously stepped into a place of not waiting for another person, or a role, or an occupation to come along and save me, rescue me, or bring me fulfillment. I stepped further back from the irrationally over-productive culture I live in and from my own overly masculine (read as yang) values that have pushed me towards constant action and achievement in the outer world. In the process of being so driven, I had unknowingly cut off vital aspects of my being. I abandoned central aspects of myself which relate to the feminine (yin) principle. Through the work with the three masks I deepened my relationship with my inner masculine principle who had at times been willing to sacrifice the feminine while on his hero's quest. Further, through releasing the existential guilt and shame that has been projected onto me, and women in general, my personal feminine qualities are being redeemed, liberated, and transformed into a new, more matured, further initiated form.

In working with the three masks described in this book, I have experienced a union of at least one pair of inner opposites, as symbolized by the appearance of the images of the hermaphrodite and the magical stone which appeared in the ritual with the Horned One mask. I believe I have actually undergone a *coniunctio*, which I am still, years later, integrating and figuring out how to articulate. I believe the masks were intrinsic to this experience, as I will summarize in the next chapter.

End Notes

1. Harding, 1980
2. von Franz, 1972
3. Fierz-David, 1980, p. xii

21 EXPLORING THE BOUNDARIES

Though I was familiar with the relationship between masks and initiation, I had not expected my personal experience with masks to, essentially, follow a process comparable to initiation. During this exploration, I was certainly being challenged to stretch beyond my known limits and expand into uncharted territory, which was bewildering and uncomfortable. Henderson[1] says that the process of initiation is often marked by a period of discomfort and disorientation and is reflected in dreams and synchronicities which correspond to the patterns of the initiation archetype. At such times, it can feel as if the ego is collapsing in on itself.

Jung instructed that during transitional periods, if the ego is strong enough and the psyche is essentially intact and whole, it will begin sending symbols of the archetypal Self to assist the fragmenting ego undergo transformation and restructure into a new, more evolved configuration. This idea directly corresponds with my experiences as induced by the masks. The symbols that appeared pointed me clearly toward the Self Archetype, and the ritual mask work helped to illustrate aspects of the individuation process - the process of aligning the ego with the Self. Throughout this investigation, I did feel as though my ego structures were breaking down, to later come back together in a new, more integrated way.

The corresponding mythic material, introduced by the mask work, helped me to structure the otherwise confusing experiences that arose. I found it incredibly helpful to know that my experiences mirrored parts of the archetypal pattern of initiation, as illustrated in the myth of Ariadne and Dionysus. Individuation can be a long and at times, confusing process that requires patience, perseverance, containment, and mirroring. Masks functioned as the container and mirror. I was able to project unconscious material onto the masks, and the masks captured and contained the projections. The masks held the unconscious material and reflected it back to me as I worked with them and contemplated the experiences. Myths emerged to provide a map of the uncharted territory I stumbled upon in my work with masks.

Plumbing the Layers

Let's return to the layers of mask work described in Chapter Eight. The first level has to do with projecting unconscious material onto the mask so that it can be contemplated and then integrated into conscious awareness. The second level is working with personal complexes through masks and the third level is working with the archetypes. Based on my experiences with the Horned One mask, I believe there may be a fourth level of experience induced by masks. This layer of work goes below the personal unconscious and beyond the collective unconscious into a realm referred to as *psychoidal*, which I explain, to the best of my understanding, below.

With the three masks described in this book, I was clearly working with projections and complexes, yet I believe that I moved beyond the personal shadow and into deeper layers of the unconscious. The archetypal symbols that came forward in the Star, Void, and Horned One masks did not strictly address my personal projections and complexes. Although that was an essential part of the process, it was not the only thing going on.

Through the masks I was able to go deeper into psyche, into cultural complex material such as the scapegoat. I moved into the third level discussed above and encountered powerful archetypal forces such as creation and destruction, which exist in a deeper layer of psyche - the collective unconscious. However, the most profound and mysterious experience occurred during the ritual with the Horned One mask, which I believe moved me to an even deeper level of mask work that has to do with the psychoidal realm.

Beyond Psyche

As described in the last few chapters, the personality that arrived in conjunction with the Horned One mask appeared to exist beyond the confines of my psyche. Its presence merged seamlessly into my conscious, waking reality. The imaginal realm overlapped with my mundane world in such a way that it was as if I were experiencing a waking dream. I experienced the spirit as being *materially present* with me, as opposed to being present only in the interior regions of my mind. The being was literally *embodied* in the mask, and its presence moved through me in an inexplicable way.

I liken the experience to those described by numerous tribal and indigenous mask workers who explain the embodiment as a type of spirit possession.[2] The best explanation I have found, so far, to help elucidate the mystery of what took place that afternoon with the horned mask, is the idea of the psychoid realm, which originated with Jung and has been expanded upon by contemporary Jungian analysts, most notably, Jeffery Raff.[3] In Depth psychology the word *psychoid* is used to describe experience in which mind and body overlap (Jung) on one end, and where mind and spirit overlap (Raff) on the other. Jung addressed the physical end of the psychoidal spectrum and Raff expands the concept out into the realm of spirit.

Jung used the term *psychoid* to refer to the area within psychic experience where mind and body, thought and matter, overlap. Within the human being, it is the place where mind and body influence and alter each other. Jung asserted that mind and matter do not exist separately but are intrinsically connected. For example, traumatic memories and knowledge of them exist not only in the mind, but are also stored somatically, in the body. Here, Jung introduced the concept of the mind-body connection into Western psychology.[4] The theory of the psychoidal realm is tricky to untangle and I am admittedly in the early stages of grasping it. I have an intuitive hunch that further research into theories of psychoid reality, which has informed and been informed by contemporary fields such as quantum physics, will further my understanding of the psychic phenomena surrounding masks.

Psyche's Spectrum

In his later writings, Jung began suggesting that the archetype exists both in the psyche and in the world at large. The non-psychic aspect of the archetype, the part that exists outside in the world, he referred to as the *psychoid archetype*. He illustrated this with the analogy of the electromagnetic spectrum. The visible part of the spectrum corresponds to the aspects of the archetype which reach the conscious mind. The invisible infrared end of the spectrum corresponds to the unconscious biological aspects of the archetype that merge with the physical. Jung suggested that archetypes not only govern the behavior of humans, but they underlie the structure of all living organisms and inorganic matter as well. According to this theory, the archetype is not merely a psychic entity, but is, more fundamentally, a link between invisible spirit and visible matter. In other words, Jung believed that archetypes exist in the psyche *and* in nature, that they shape the mind *as well as* matter.

Jung applied the term *unus mundus* to his notion of a unitary reality that underlies the manifest world. He regarded archetypes as the mediators of the *unus mundus*, not only organizing ideas in the psyche, but also as being the fundamental organizing principle behind matter and energy.[5] In basic terms, Jung proposed that archetypes are primary forces which play a central role in the creation of the human mind as well as the physical world itself. Jung laid the foundation for later theories on the psychoid realm that move into exploring the places where the human psyche meets spirit. Jungian analyst Robert Romanyshyn[6] describes the phenomenon of psychoid reality as spirit infused in matter, as conceived by the early alchemists. It is interesting to note that his description brings into play an idea that arose with the Guiding Light mask, the idea that the spark of light is a symbol of the alchemical "light of nature," also known as the spirit in matter.

> The psychoid archetype is the anima mundi, the soul of the world. In his essay Jung gives a long description of how the alchemists described the soul of the world as a multitude of fiery sparks... Those 'fiery sparks' are what were once called the '*lumen naturae*', the light of nature. With the psychoid

archetype, then, the unconscious at the foundation of depth psychology turns out to be the consciousness of nature. In the psychoidal depths where psyche and nature are one, in the unus mundus the complex human psyche is led back to nature and as such is led back to its nature. In this regard the broken connection between mind and matter…is addressed.

From Psyche to Psychoid

At this point, I cannot explain the mysterious encounter with the Horned One mask. However, I have found that Jeffrey Raff[7] provides a theoretical model which warrants further exploration in regard to explaining the phenomenon of the spirit behind the mask. He takes Jung's idea of the psychoidal and extends it along the other end of the metaphoric light spectrum, moving away from the infrared area of matter, across the visible spectrum, to the ultraviolet end which represents the realm of spirit. For Raff, the psychoid realm includes experiences of a mystical nature, which is an area usually relegated to spirituality and religion.

Examining the notion of spirit from a psychological standpoint has the potential to introduce a mire of philosophical and theological confusion. Jung, himself, was careful to examine spirit in terms of how it intersects with psyche and to steer away from spiritual and metaphysical opining. A survey of Jung's theories on the human spirit would take this discussion too far afield. Suffice it to say, Jung observed a psychological need in his patients, colleagues, and even in himself, to address the very real experiences that fall within the realm of what is typically considered mystical and spiritual.[8]

Raff[9] writes extensively about the psychoidal realm as an intermediate realm that lies between psyche and matter and is akin to what traditional societies referred to as the spirit realm. He postulates that this intermediary realm is populated with autonomous beings, much like the archetypes of the collective unconscious. However, unlike the traditional notion of archetypes, psychoidal beings exist independent of the human psyche. Raff[10] draws this idea from Jung's theories on psychoid archetypes, from his work with active imagination, and from the work of the Sufi mystic Ibn 'Arabi, who lived some nine hundred years ago.

At this writing, I am still trying to tease apart the difference between an archetype and a psychoidal being. It seems to me that Raff's definition of psychoidal beings is similar to Jung's description of psychoid archetypes, as delineated above. From my preliminary understanding it seems that the collective unconscious, from which the archetypes emanate, is seen as existing within the human psyche whereas psychoidal beings come from a realm beyond the human psyche, which Raff[11] affiliates with the spirit realm and even with divinity. It seems that Raff also draws a rough parallel between the imaginal realm and the spirit realm. In his model, there are imaginal experiences which take place within the psyche, and there are imaginal experiences that take place on an exterior imaginal or subtle realm which he refers to as psychoidal. Jung[12], in his examination of the alchemical model of spirit in matter, hints at the subtle realm Raff refers to:

> It always remains an obscure point whether the ultimate transformations in the alchemical process ought to be sought more in the material or more in the spiritual realm. Actually, however, the question is wrongly put: there was no 'either or' for that age, but there did exist an intermediate realm between mind and matter, i.e., a psychic realm of subtle bodies whose characteristic it is to manifest themselves in mental as well as material form. This is the only view that makes sense of alchemical ways of thought which must otherwise appear non-sensical.

Raff's other major influence, 'Arabi, wrote about distinct layers of imagination, where different types of mystical and visionary experiences take place. In this model, the psychoidal experience is one in which the symbol and the interaction with it take place in an imaginal reality that exists independent of the human psyche. Raff[13] describes this aspect of the psychoidal realm in the following way:

> One can experience inner figures in many ways. Active imagination connects individuals with inner

figures which, while very powerful, are clearly imaginal and derived from the psyche. These figures feel as if they were coming from within oneself. Typically, one experiences them with eyes closed and attention directed inward. They are the psychic figures which personify the forces of the unconscious. However, every so often, one may experience a figure that *feels* completely different. This figure feels as if it were coming from outside oneself, as if it existed in the external world, in the room in which one finds oneself, for example. One's eyes are open and the felt sense is that one perceives a figure that does *not* come from within. The attention of the ego is focused outward, not inward. These are the experiences I refer to using the term 'psychoid.'

Essentially, Raff hypothesizes that there may be two types of figures that can appear to us: those that originate within the human psyche, such as archetypes, and those that derive from the psychoid realm. He proposes that a psychoidal being can assume form within the psyche and manifest as an inner image that exactly mirrors the psychoidal entity which exists outside of the psyche. Raff[14] elaborates on this notion:

> There is no difference between the spiritual being itself and the imaginal form in which one experiences it. Active imagination with such a figure therefore relates one to the world beyond the psyche, to the spiritual domain and reality in which the divine resides. Though it may never be possible to experience that reality in and of itself, one can experience it through the form it assumes.

I cannot say for certain that the presence I experienced while working with the Horned One mask was a psychoidal entity, or psychoid archetype. What I do know is that the experience I had seems to match Raff's description of psychoidal experiences quite well, in that the imaginal figure felt as if it did not come from within. It seemed to come from outside of me and exist in the external, rather than the internal world. I know that the *feeling* I had during the ritual was quite different from the feeling of previous experiences and that my conscious mind was focused outward, into the room, rather than inward. I do not yet have a clear answer to what occurred. This is an area I will continue exploring to see if I can glean further insights into the mysterious spirit beings which seem to inhabit masks and the powerful experiences that accompany the embodiment of said spirits.

In order to keep this project manageable, I had to narrow my scope as much as possible. While this book gives a basic picture of my experiences, there was much more taking place, both experientially and in terms of my research. However, it would have been impossible to include it all within the limits of this document. I believe that the work I have done on this project can open new doors of investigation into many areas of future study including: masks and neuropsychology; masks and somatic psychology studies; and the role of play and the ludic (play-oriented) centers of the brain in mask work (which I believe are ruled in part by the Dionysian principle), to name just a few.

Coming Full Circle

At this point, I can confidently say that the work herein is about masks as a tool and a container for transformation as expressed in the contemporary initiation process which, in depth psychology, is known as individuation. This is at the heart of my work and is central to my work with masks. Individuation is about becoming a unique expression of the vast human potential. It is about changing from one merged with the world, fragmented and pulled this way and that by internal and external forces, through a complete transformation into an integrated and liberated personality. This is the only true foundation one can rest on – a true and clear sense of self as an inimitable being.[15] Jung[16] clarifies the importance of individuation:

> Life that just happens in and for itself is not real life; it is real only when it is *known*. Only a unified personality can experience life, not that personality

which is split up into partial aspects, that bundle of odds and ends which also calls itself a 'man.'

I like to think that my experiences with masks connect me to the larger continuum of human encounters with the mystery and power of the mask. I wholeheartedly believe that masks are a perfectly suited medium for exploring the boundaries between inner and outer, self and other, the known and the unknown, and that in this way, masks are intrinsically linked to the archetypal forces represented by the Trickster. At the beginning of this book, I put forth the idea that masks have the power to help us integrate important personal and collective stories of duality and ambiguity – stories of intense pain intertwined with immense strength, beauty, and joy. At the close of this investigation, I unwaveringly stand by my conviction that masks hold the potential to reconnect us with our mythic roots and with the very essence of what it means to be human.

Approaching with Respect, Patience and Humility

Depth-oriented ritual mask work may not be for everyone. But for those with whom it does resonate, I encourage proceeding with humility, mindfulness, and the requisite caution that should accompany any foray into the unconscious. Although referred to as imaginal, this work is very real and very powerful and should be undertaken with an understanding of this fact. That said, there are myriad ways to approach this type of deep work with psyche. For me, the mask captivated my attention and moved me forward along my own path, pushing me toward new realms and exciting new horizons.

A clear limitation to this type of work is that it is so individualized, and guided by the unconscious, that it can be difficult to predict and standardize. The distinctively personal approach to self-awareness embraced by depth psychology is often obscure. I have found that with patience and perseverance the convolutions slowly begin to unwind and the concealed path to wholeness eventually becomes revealed in a manner unique to each person. The results will vary from person to person, and each consecutive experience had by one individual will likely vary, making it difficult, if not impossible to quantify. However, qualitative changes can be *experienced* by the subject. In my case, the changes were *observed* by those who know me. My husband, sons, friends, and especially my therapist, witnessed the changes in my feelings, belief structures, and behaviors resulting from my work with masks.

Ritual mask work has helped me to better understand my own process of individuation. I believe this work has been, in essence, about reconciling the dark and light in my life, in my history, and ultimately, in my psyche. It has been about moving beyond the duality that has pinned me down to a limited experience of myself and my reality. It has taught me *experientially,* what it means to align my ego with my Self - without attachment or inflation. The work with masks has helped me to create enough distance from my personal wounds so that I am no longer overwhelmed by the idea of sharing creative work that stems from them.

This project has opened up an area of passionate interest and has inspired me to continue my investigations beyond this project and to continue developing the masking methods I teach to others. Beyond all of that, this work has transformed me in profound and unfathomable ways that I am only beginning to understand and am not yet able to articulate. The depth and complexity of this work, which taps into mysterious realms that have an inexplicable yet palpable impact on psyche and soma, is difficult to convey.

I imagine that the greatest depth psychologists, such as Jung and von Franz, would advise that the best thing to do when attempting a task such as this is to look inside for guidance. In my quest to understand the power of the mask, I am looking for signposts as they surface from my own unconscious. I have long believed that the answers I seek reside within. I am continually amazed by the innate intelligence of the psyche and I agree with the depth perspective which holds that psyche itself is the best guide and teacher. As I end this phase of my journey with masks I am filled with gratitude for the work that has stemmed from this investigation. I believe that this is only the beginning of a lifetime worth of work that has arisen from the depths of my own being. I will leave the reader with the encouragement and caution found in Jung's Red Book[17] which has inspired me forward through the inevitable confusion that arises when one is forging one's own path into the hinterlands of uncharted territory:

Woe betide those who live by way of examples! Life is not with them. If you live according to an example, you thus live the life of that example, but who should live your own life if not yourself? So live yourselves…The way is within us, but not in Gods, nor in teachings, nor in laws. Within us is the way, the truth, and the life.

End Notes

1. Henderson, 1967
2. De Jong, 1999; Phillips, 1978)
3. Raff 2000, 2003
4. Samuels, Shorter, & Plaut, 2003
5. Jung, 1963
6. Romanyshan, 2009, para. 6
7. Raff 2000, 2003
8. Hopcke, 1989; Raff, 2000
9. Raff 2000, 2003
10. Raff 2000
11. Raff 2000
12. Jung, 1965, para. 394
13. Raff 2000, p. 28 -29
14. Raff 2000, p. 31
15. Jung, 2009; Fierz-David, 1980; Stein 1996
16. Jung, as quoted in Fierz-David, 1980, p. 16-17
17. Jung, 2009, p. 231

APPENDIX A

TRANSCRIPT OF DIALOGUE WITH THE GUIDE

My awareness is pulled up into the night sky and I have the perspective of being a star out in space, looking down on the Earth. The Earth appears in my mind's eye as a spinning ball of matter, always in motion.

I hear: *"There's no standing still. The universe is always in motion. The planets are in motion, spinning and circling. It's an illusion that you are standing still on the face of the earth, standing still on a flat surface; which is what your senses tell you. It's always moving. There's always balance. Balance is the law of the universe. The law of balance…"*

I have a hard time staying with the experience. It's hard for my ego to surrender to what's occurring and to look at my world from this distant and more expansive perspective. It frightens me to hold an awareness of the existence of forces so much greater than me. I'm overcome with a feeling of insignificance. I start thinking that, in the face of it all; I am but a tiny blip on the cosmic radar…totally insignificant, as all 6.5+ billion of us humans are.

I return my attention to the Guide and to what it is showing me. I hear: *"I am this one out here in space. You've seen me before. I've brought you here before.* (I think of dreams from my childhood). *I am connected to something much larger than you, and I am part of you. You are on earth, in your body, but your consciousness is also up here."*

I am looking down on the earth from a great distance, still frightened. I feel alone and isolated in the blackness. My existence seems so fragile. My thoughts stretch out into a web of associations: spirit in matter, consciousness in matter, moving in and out of matter at will. Consciousness enlivening and inhabiting matter – consciously inhabiting matter, moving in and out of matter – that is the shape shifter.

I feel myself, my ego identity and body, and I also feel the spark of light, the spark of consciousness and life force and I realize that I am all of these things simultaneously. I feel a strange warming sensation in my body and I wonder aloud into the tape recorder: "Are my soul and ego uniting in a *coniunctio*? Is that what's happening right now?"

I am aware of both myself and the Other. I feel a tingling on top of my head, it moves all the way down my body. It feels like pulses of strong energy moving through me. A profound visual and kinesthetic experience is taking place. I struggle to stay fully grounded in my conscious awareness. I realize that I am deepening into an altered state of awareness so I pull out of it and solidly into my ego awareness so that I can continue tracking the experience. I decide to ask it, the star being a question.

I ask it: "Why are you the Guide, *my* Guide?"

It says: *"I am the guide because I hold wisdom of the spheres, of the planes, of all the realms, of existence.*
I am the guide because I know the layout of the architecture of the universe, although I am not the architect.
I am the guide through the architecture. This is my purpose.
This is my wisdom; the wisdom of the realms and the planes of existence.
I am wise to the laws of the universe. I am beyond the laws of the universe.
I exist outside the laws of the universe.
I am the spark of light for which you have many names.
Spark of creation, divine spark, radiated from the one from the unity, in infinite pieces.
I exist as the one, the whole and the many
All at once...simultaneously
I am the one who holds this in balance...
The individuality and the unity, the one and the many
I can move between them both, hold them both, balance them both, work with them both, see and understand, and master them both
I understand the laws of them both, the laws that bind them together in this homeostasis."

It goes on:
"I am ambiguous, not about good and evil, light and dark. I am the divine spark that moves in and out of matter. My function is neither good nor evil and is therefore ambiguous.

It just is. I just am.
Without qualifiers.
I am part of everything and I hold this knowledge of being part of everything in my consciousness.
I remember this.
Unlike you, I don't know how to see myself as truly separate. I see no separation. I understand that the boundaries are illusions. Just as time and space are illusions.
And yet, they all exist: time and space and boundaries….in this great paradox…that I am a part of…that I am the center of.
This is what I bring to you. This is one of the many lessons I bring you, so that you can understand more about whom I am…who you are.
I bring you a higher perspective that is sometimes joyous and beautiful for you and sometimes harsh and painful for you.
I simply show you what is.
I can be a mirror for you, reflecting what is.
Helping you open yourself to it.

The star-being continues:

"You called me in to help you integrate all the fragments, to embody your Self, to embody the divine spark, to teach you how to be, consciously be this divine spark in matter…holding unity consciousness while being separate…Walking that balance holding that balance…Living in the constant meeting of the opposites and the constant transformation that occurs – being aware of it, seeing it, being able to communicate and articulate it, allowing the guidance to come and move you. It's not right, not wrong, it just is."

"In my mirror you will see many things, things that may frighten you, things that may delight you. I will help you. I will guide you to be able to hold what's in the mirror, to be able to look into the mirror and see the reality that's reflected there. I will help you do this."

TRANSCRIPT OF ACTIVE IMAGINATION WITH THE VOID

As soon as I entered into the active imagination with the being behind the black mask, it began speaking to me. Following is our dialogue that took place in this first active imagination with the Void mask spirit.

"I am the mystery…yes of death and the great yawning void
I am not only the unknown, but the absence of the known
I am a vast emptiness that stretches before you, the emptiness you feared
up in space.
I was there with you and the star.
We are, in truth, inseparable, the Star and I.

T: but right now I am seeking to separate you. That seems to be my task…

Yes, to separate who we are IN YOU. That can be done, to a point.
But you will see, when you reach deeply into me, you find her. When you
enter fully into her, you find me.
Are you ready for this? Can you handle this paradox?

T: I'm not sure. It doesn't really make sense to me.

In time it will.
I am not what you were expecting, am I?

T: I'm not sure. I feel confused right now. I don't think so. I guess I was expecting a monster, a devil, a demon, something horrifying.

You really don't understand me at all, do you?

T: I guess not. Can I make a mask of you and work with you through masked ritual performance? Would that be okay?

Do you really think you're ready for this? For me?

T: I'm not sure

You better be sure.

T: what will happen if I'm not?
I will devour you, dismember you. I will rip you to shreds and eat you piece by piece until you become me.

T: No, that won't do. I'm not going to allow that. It seems like you're just showing up, like you want to be worked with, like you're following me even.

I'm not following you. I'm following her, following your precious star, the spark you are so taken by, so enamored with. Wherever she is, so am I.

T: so if I'm working with her, how can I not work with you?

You cannot not work with me.

T: then I must be ready, because here you both are.

It's laughing now, this spirit.
You have no idea what you're getting yourself into here, do you?

T: why don't you tell me?

You think you want to understand the mysteries of the universe, the secrets of life and death. Do you think you are ready for this?

T: What I'm trying to understand is myself, my own unconscious. I want to integrate the fragments of my own psyche.

Then why call in the archetypes, as you call us? Why dip your hand into the well of the gods if it is simply self-knowledge you seek?

T: because you are in me. You are in my psyche. To know myself I must know you.

How do you know this? Because you read it in books? Do you think your studies make you wise?

T: No, because I <u>experience</u> this. I've always experienced this. I am experiencing it right now. My studies help me understand. But they're not enough. They don't fully illuminate my inner reality. That is why I'm doing this work with masks. Because you all seem to want a voice. You seem to WANT to be known, understood, heard, seen, and expressed. Or am I wrong about this?

No, not wrong. But you're not right either. You're right that your understanding is limited. You're right that we're a part of you, because we are a part of everything. It is you who want to understand us. We do not need to be understood. My existence does not depend on your awareness of me. It is not my desires that bring me here, but yours.

T: Perhaps. Can I work with you without being broken into bits? I've been broken so many times. What I seek now is repair. I want mending. I want to piece myself back together and I'm not sure I can do it without you. You seem to be a piece of my puzzle, a color in my mosaic. Yes, I suppose I do desire to understand you, but not to be torn apart in the process.

Even if more tearing is required?

T: is it?

What do you think?

T: I'm not sure.

So many questions. So much uncertainty. What do you want with all of this work you seem to think is so important? What are you expecting to gain? What are your intentions? You would be wise to answer these questions before proceeding.

T: Perhaps it is in proceeding that I will find the answers.

Perhaps. But you better be certain you are ready for this, for the answers you seek.

T: Can you help me answer them?

Yes I can. If you are ready, I can help you.

T: How will I know if I'm ready?

You will know at the very core of your being when you're ready.

T: I think I am ready and maybe the confusion is really just fear.

Yes.

T: Do you think I'm ready?
Only you can answer this. It has to come from you.

T: Yes, I am ready. I command this be done with ease and with grace; that it be well contained and made digestible; that it is given to me in a way I can understand and integrate; that it be done in alignment with my highest and best and the highest and best of all; that it's manageable; that I can step into and out of it at will. If all these conditions are met, then yes, I am ready.

So it shall be.

T: Will you please show me your mask?

All I see is a great gaping void.

I end the active imagination.

APPENDIX C

PRAYER STICK USED IN HORNED ONE MASK RITUAL

Figure 16. Prayer Stick Front

Figure 17. Prayer Stick Back

APPENDIX D

DRAWING THAT APPEARED IN HORNED ONE MASK RITUAL

Figure 18. Venus of Willendorf Drawing

APPENDIX E

QUARTZ CRYSTAL ANCESTOR STONES THAT APPEARED IN HORNED ONE MASK RITUAL

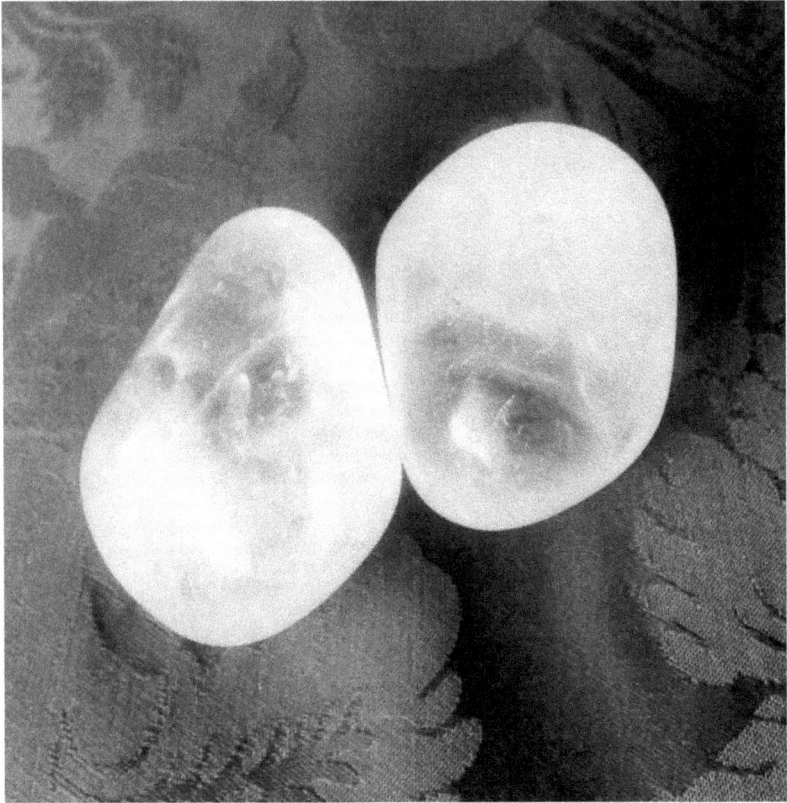

APPENDIX F

MURAL SERIES IN INITIATION HALL OF VILLA OF MYSTERIES, POMPEII

Figure 19. Initiation Hall Mural Scenes 1 - 4

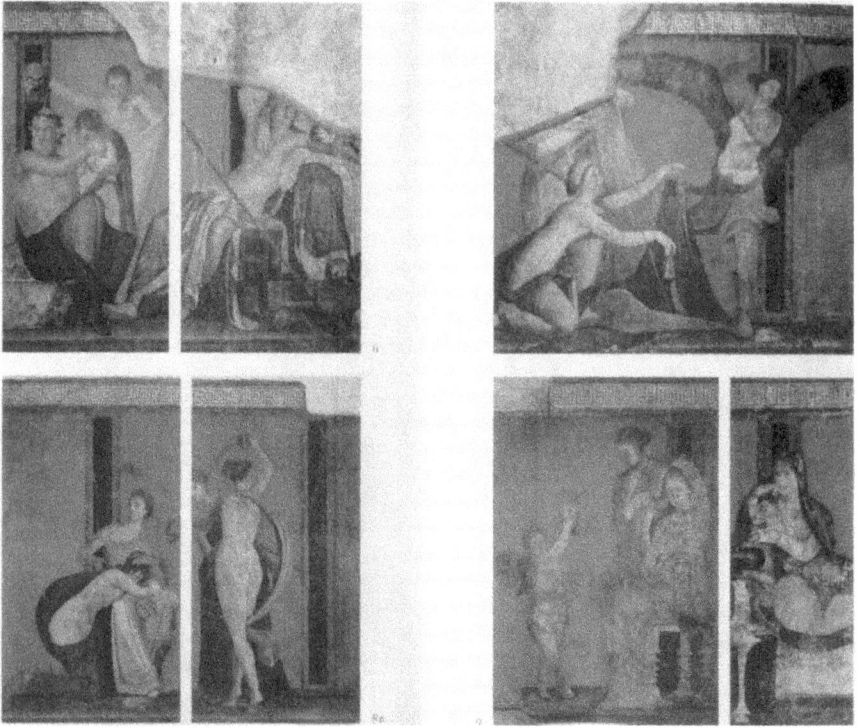

Figure 20. Initiation Hall Mural Scenes 5 - 10

GLOSSARY OF TERMS

Archetypes - latent potentials of the human psyche. Innate patterns of human experience and behavior. The inheritance at birth of the totality of human psychological and emotional potential. Universal blue prints of human experience. It is not the content, but rather, the mold that the personal, individual experience is poured into. (The Mother, The Father, The Child, etc.)

Collective Unconscious - the deepest layer of the unconscious which is innate, shared by all humanity across times and cultures, and can never be totally assimilated into consciousness. It is vast, undifferentiated, transpersonal, and composed of archetypes.

Complex - emotionally charged unconscious psychic content. (Think inferiority /superiority complex). Complexes are made of personal unconscious material which is magnetized to an archetypal core. They tend to operate autonomously, interfering with the conscious will of the ego. It's as if they have a personality of their own which can suddenly and unexpectedly overtake us and override conscious intent.

Ego - the center of the conscious, individual awareness of identity – the personal sense of "I".

Individuation - The process of integrating of all of the parts of personality into a unified whole. Psychological initiation into a state of maturity and self-actualization. The lifelong process of realizing one's potentials. Known by mystics as the state of *enlightenment.*

Persona (Personnae)- the term derives from the Latin word for masks worn by ancient actors to indicate the particular role they played. It/they function as mediators between the individual ego and society. This is not a disguise but is an identifier.

Psyche - the totality of all psychological content, conscious and unconscious. The psyche can be described as the central hub of cognition, emotions, behavior, and even the intelligence of the physical body.

Psychoidal – and esoteric term that seeks to describe aspects of the psyche that exist outside and beyond the individual's conscious and unconscious minds, such as the parts of psychic experience that move into the adjacent realms of matter and spirit.

Self - the central archetype that embodies a drive or urge to consciousness and wholeness of the personality. It is the unified center, the integrated totality of psyche (conscious and unconscious). It is a force that drives towards the full realization of the individual, and also the goal of that force.

Shadow - the dark side of the ego made up of the unknown and undeveloped. It's the most accessible layer of the unconscious. It can be made partially conscious, integrated, and transformed. It consists of forgotten and repressed contents derived from personal experiences that are incompatible with the conscious point of view. It also consists of unconscious positive potential.

Unconscious - consists of psychological (or "psychic," including, somatic, emotional, etc.) content outside of immediate awareness. There are two layers of the unconscious: the *personal* and the *collective*. The personal unconscious consists of repressed, unregistered, or simply unknown content derived from an individual's experiences.

*This list of terms has been derived and adapted from many sources over the years and serves as a hand-out to students in my advanced classes.

REFERENCES

Adler, J. (2002). *Offering from the conscious body: The discipline of authentic movement.* Rochester, VT: Inner Traditions.

Allen, T. & Phillips, C. (2000). *Myth and mankind.* London: Duncan Baird Publishers.

Archive for Research in Archetypal Symbolism (ARAS). (n.d.) ARAS Record 3Ja.174 Retrieved from: http://aras.org/.

Black, M. & Mitchell, S.A. (1995). *Freud and beyond: A history of psychoanalytic thought.* Cambridge, MA: Basic Books

Bond, D.S. (1993). *Living myth: Personal meaning as a way of life.* Boston: Shambhala Publications.

Braud, W. & Anderson, R. (1998). *Transpersonal research methods for the social sciences: Honoring human experience.* Thousand Oaks, CA: Sage Publications.

Campbell, J. (1964). *Occidental mythology: The masks of god.* New York: Penguin Compass.

Campbell, J. (1968). *The hero with a thousand faces.* Princeton, NJ: Princeton University Press.

Ching, K. & Ching, E.D. (2006). *Faces of your soul: Rituals in art, maskmaking, and guided imagery with ancestors, spirit guides, and totem animals.* Berkeley, CA: North Atlantic Books.

Chodorow, J. (1997) Introduction. *Jung on Active Imagination.* Princeton, NJ: Princeton University Press.

Christen, K. (1998). *Clowns & Tricksters: An encyclopedia of tradition and culture.* Santa Barbara, CA: ABC-CLIO Inc.

Colman, D. (1996). *Up from scapegoating: Awakening consciousness in groups.* Willamette, IL: Chiron Publications.

Coombs, A. & Holland, H. (1990). *Synchronicity; Science, myth, and the Trickster*. New York: Paragon House.

Coppin, J. & Nelson, E. (2005). *The art of inquiry: A depth psychological perspective*. Putnam, CT: Spring Publications.

De Jong, F. (1999). Trajectories of a mask performance: The case of the Senegalese Kumpo. *Cahiers d'Études Africaines*, Vol. 39, Cahier 153), pg. 49-7. Paris: EHESS. Retrieved from: http://www.jstor.org/stable/4392913.

Deutsch, H. (1969). *A psychoanalytic study of the myth of Dionysus and Apollo: Two variants of the son-mother relationship*. New York: International Universities Press.

Eck, D. (1981). *Darsan: Seeing the divine image in India*. New York: Columbia University Press.

Edinger, E. (1991). *Anatomy of the psyche: Alchemical symbolism in psychotherapy*. Peru, IL: Open Court Publishing Company.

Edinger, E. (1994). *The Mysterium Lecture's: A Journey through C.G. Jung's Mysterium Coniunctionis*. Toronto: Inner City Books.

Edinger, E. (1994). *The eternal drama: The inner meaning of Greek mythology*. Boston: Shambhala Publications, Inc.

Ehrenreich, B. (2006). *Dancing in the streets: A history of collective joy*. New York: Henry Holt and Company, LLC.

Eliade, M. (1954). W. R. Trask, Trans. *The myth of the eternal return*. New York: Pantheon Books.

Eliade, M. (1963). *Myth and reality*. New York: Harper & Row.

Elston, K.D. (2004). Ritual and inhabiting the mask: An actor's search for the transcendent creative state. *The Journal of Religion and Theatre*, Vol. 3, No. 2, Fall 2004.

http://www.rtjournal.org/vol_3/no_2/elston.html. ISSN 1544-8762.

Emigh, J. (1996). *Masked performance: The play of self and other in ritual and theatre*. Philadelphia: University of Pennsylvania Press.

Essential Science Publishers. (2000). *Essential oils desk reference.*

Faris, J.C. (1990). *The nightway.* Albuquerque, NM: University of New Mexico Press.

Feinstein, D. & Krippner, S. (1988). *Personal mythology: The psychology of your evolving self: using ritual, dreams, and imagination to discover your inner story.* Los Angeles: J.P. Tarcher, Inc.

Fierz-David, L. (1980). G. Phelan, Trans. *Women's Dionysian initiation: the Villa of Mysteries in Pompeii.* Dallas, TX: Spring Publications.

Foster, S. & Little, M. (1992). *The book of the vision quest: Personal transformation in the wilderness.* New York: Fireside.

Freke, T. & Gandy, P. (2001). *Jesus and the lost goddess: The original teachings of the original Christians.* New York: Three Rivers Press.

Freud, S. & Gay, P. (Ed). (1989). *The Freud Reader.* New York: W.W. Norton.

Gazda, E.K. (Ed). (2000). *The Villa of Mysteries in Pompeii: Ancient ritual – modern muse.* Ann Arbor, MI: The University of Michigan Museum of Art.

Gendlin, E. (1986). *Let your body interpret your dreams.* Wilmette, IL: Chiron Publications

Gimbutas, M. (1991). *The civilization of the goddess: The world of old Europe.* New York: HarperCollins Publishers.

Hall, N. (1988). *Those women.* Dallas, TX: Spring Publications, Inc.

Halifax, J. (1982). *Shaman: The wounded healer.* New York: Crossroad.

Henderson, J. & Sherwood, D. (2003). *Transformation of the psyche: The symbolic alchemy of the Splendor Solis.* New York: Routledge.

Henderson, J. (1967, 2005). *Thresholds of initiation.* Willamette, IL: Chiron Publications.

Hill, G. (1992). *Masculine and feminine: The natural flow of opposites in the psyche.* Boston: Shambhala Publications, Inc.

Hillman, J. (1975/1992). *Re-visioning psychology.* New York: HarperPerennial.

Hillman, J. (1979). *The dream and the underworld.* New York: HarperCollins Publishers Inc.

Hillman, J. (1983/2009). *Healing fiction.* Putnam, CT: Spring Publications.

Hillman, J. (2004). *Archetypal Psychology.* Putnam, CT: Spring Publications.

Hoeller, S.A. (2002) *Gnosticism: New light on the ancient tradition of inner knowing.* Wheaton, IL: The Theosophical Publishing House.

Hollis, J. (1996). *Swamplands of the Soul.* Toronto: Inner City Books.

Hollis, J. (2000). *The archetypal imagination.* College Station, TX: Texas A&M University Press.

Hopcke, R. H. (1991). N. Shwartz-Salant & M. Stein, (Eds.), On the threshold of change: Symbolization and transitional space. *Liminality and transitional phenomena.* Willamette, IL: Chiron Publications.

Hopcke, R.H. (1989). *A guided tour of the collected works of C. G. Jung.* Boston: Shambhala Publications, Inc.

Hyde, L. (1998). *Trickster makes this world; Mischief, myth and art.* New York: Farrar, Straus, and Giroux.

Jensen, B. (2001). *Mandorla: Ancient symbol of wholeness.* Journal of Sandplay Therapists of America. Retrieved from: http://www.sandplay.org/symbols/mandorla.htm.

Johnson, R. (1986). *Inner work: Using dreams and active imagination for personal* growth. San Francisco: HarperCollins Publishers.

Johnstone, K. (1979). *Impro: Improvisation and the theater.* New York: Theater Arts Books.

Jung, C.G. (1916/1958). (R.F.C. Hull, Trans.). *The transcendent function.* In H. Read, M. Fordham, G. Adler, & W. McGuire, (Eds.), *The collected works of C. G. Jung.* (Vol. 8). Princeton, NJ: Princeton University Press.

Jung, C.G. (1930-1934/1997**).** C. Douglas (Ed.),*Visions: Notes of the seminar given in 1930-1934 by C.G. Jung.* Princeton, NJ: Princeton University Press.

Jung, C. G. (1938). *Psychology and religion.* New Haven, CT: Yale University Press.

Jung, C.G. (1945/1967). (R.F.C. Hull, Trans.). *Alchemical studies.* . In H. Read, M. Fordham, G. Adler, & W. McGuire, (Eds.), *The collected works of C. G. Jung.* Bollingen Series 20. (Vol. 11). Princeton, NJ: Princeton University Press.

Jung, C. G., (1953). (R.F.C. Hull, Trans.). *The archetypes of the collective unconscious.* In Read, H., Fordham, M., Adler, G. & W. McGuire, (Eds.), *The collected works of C.G. Jung.* (Vol. 6). New York: Pantheon Books.

Jung, C. G. (1954). (R.F.C. Hull, Trans.). *Psychological types.* In H. Read, M. Fordham, G. Adler, & W. McGuire, (Eds.), *The collected works of C. G. Jung.* Bollingen Series 20. (Vol. 5). Princeton, NJ: Princeton University Press.

Jung, C.G. (1955). *The interpretation of nature and the psyche: Synchronicity: An acausal connecting principle.* New York: Pantheon Books.

Jung, C.G. (1957/2010). (R.F.C. Hull, Trans.). *Answer to Job.* In H. Read, M. Fordham, G. Adler, & W. McGuire, (Eds.), *The collected works of C. G. Jung.* Bollingen Paperback Series. (Vol. 11). Princeton, NJ: Princeton University Press.

Jung, C.G. (1959/1993). V. Staub de Laszlo (Ed.), *The basic writings of C.G. Jung.* New York: Random House.

Jung, C.G. (1963/1970). H. Read, M. Fordham, G. Adler, & W. McGuire, (Eds.), *Mysterium coniunctionis: An inquiry into the separation and synthesis of the psychic opposites in alchemy.* Princeton, NJ: Princeton University Press.

Jung, C.G. (1964). *Man and his symbols.* New York: Dell.

Jung, C.G. (1965). (R.F.C. Hull, Trans.). *Psychology and alchemy.* In H. Read, M. Fordham, G. Adler, & W. McGuire, (Eds.), *The collected works of C. G. Jung.* Bollingen Paperback Series 20. (Vol. 12). Princeton, NJ: Princeton University Press.

Jung, C.G. (1967). (R.F.C.Hull, Trans.) *Alchemical studies.* In H. Read, M. Fordham, G. Adler, & W. McGuire, (Eds.), *The collected works of C. G. Jung.* Bollingen Series 20. (Vol. 13). Princeton, NJ: Princeton University Press.

Jung, C.G. (1961). *Memories, dreams, and reflections.* New York: Random House, Inc.

Jung, C.G. (1971). J. Campbell (Ed.), *The portable Jung.* New York: Penguin Books USA Inc.

Jung, C. G. (1977). (R.F.C. Hull, Trans.). *Symbols of Transformation.* In H. Read, M. Fordham, G. Adler, & W. McGuire, (Eds.), *The collected works of C. G. Jung.* Bollingen Series 20. (Vol. 5). Princeton, NJ: Princeton University Press.

Jung, C.G. (1997). J. Chodorow (Ed.), *Jung on Active Imagination.* Princeton, NJ: Princeton University Press.

Jung, C. & Sabini, M. (2002). *The Earth Has a Soul: The nature writings of C.G. Jung.* Berkeley, CA: North Atlantic Books.

Kalsched, D. (1996/2005) *The inner world of trauma: Archetypal defenses of the personal spirit.* New York: Routledge.

Kalweit, H. (1984). *Dreamtime and inner space: The world of the shaman.* London: Shambhala Publications, Inc.

Kerenyi, K. (1960). R. Bernoulli (Ed). *Spiritual disciplines: Papers from the Eranos Yearbooks.* Princeton, NJ: Princeton University Press.

Kerenyi, K. (1976). *Dionysos: Archetypal image of the indestructable life.* Princeton, N.J. Princeton University Press.

Kerenyi, K. (1986). *Hermes, guide of souls: The mythologem of the masculine source of life.* Dallas, TX: Spring Publications.

King James Version Holy Bible (1978). Regency Publishing House.

Larsen, S. (1990). *The mythic imagination: The quest for meaning through personal mythology.* New York: Bantam Books.

Lawrence, D.H. (1921-1922/2004). B. Steele (Ed.), *Psychoanalysis and the unconscious and fantasia of the unconscious.* Cambridge, MA. Cambridge University Press.

Layton, B. (1987). *The Gnostic scriptures: Ancient wisdom for the new age.* New York: Doubleday.

Leonard, L.S. (1982). *The wounded woman: Healing the father-daughter relationship.* Boulder, CO: Shambhala Publications, Inc.

Lévi-Strauss, C. (1982). *The way of the masks.* Seattle: University of Washington Press.

Liddell, H.G, & Scott, R. (n.d.) *A Greek – English lexicon.* Boston, MA: Tufts University. Retrieved from: http://www.perseus.tufts.edu/hopper/text?doc=Perseus%3 Atext%3A1999.04.0057%3Aentry%3Dyuxopompo%2Fs.

Long, C. (1963). *Alpha: The myths of creation.* Toronto: Collier-MacMillan Canada, Inc.

Mahdi, L.C., Foster, S., & Little, M. (1987). *Betwixt & between: Patterns of masculine and feminine initiation.* La Salle, IL: Open Court.

Malchiodi, K. (2002). *The soul's palette: Drawing on art's transformative powers for health and well-being.* Boston: Shambhala Publications.

Matthews, C. (1991/2001). *Sophia: Goddess of wisdom, bride of god.* Wheaton, IL: The Theosophical Publishing House.

Matthews, W. (1902/1995). *The Night Chant: A Navaho ceremony.* New York: Knickerbocker Press.

McLean, A. (1989/2002). *The alchemical mandala: A survey of the mandala in Western esoteric traditions.* Grand Rapids, MI: Phanes Press, Inc.

McNiff, S. (1998). *Art-based research.* London: Jessica Kingsley Publishers.

McNiff, S. (2004). *Art heals: How creativity cures the soul.* Boston: Shambhala Publications.

Mead, G.R.S. (1921/2005). *Pistis Sophia: The Gnostic tradition of Mary Magdalene, Jesus, and his disciples.* New York: Dover Publications, Inc.

Mellick, J. (1996). *The art of dreaming: Tools for creative dream work.* Berkeley, CA: Conari Press.

Merriam – Webster (1973) *Webster's new collegiate dictionary.* Springfield, MA: C. & G. Merriam Co.

Moore, T. (1992). *Care of the soul: A guide for cultivating depth and sacredness in everyday life.* New York: Harper Perennial.

Mosak, H.H. (Ed). (1973). *Alfred Adler: His influence on psychology today.* Park Ridge, NJ: Noyes Press.

Moustakas, C. (1990). *Heuristic research: Design, methodology, and applications.* Newbury Park, CA: Sage Publications, Inc.

Napier, D.A., (1986). *Masks, transformation, and paradox.* Berkeley, CA: University of California Press.

Neumann, E. (1955/1974). R. Manheim (Trans). *The great mother: An analysis of the archetype.* Princeton, NJ: Princeton University Press.

Neumann, E. (1969, 1990). *Depth psychology and a new ethic.* Boston: Shambhala Publications, Inc.

Nichols, S. (1980). *Jung and the tarot: An archetypal journey.* York Beach, ME: Samuel Weiser, Inc.

Nunley, J.W. & McCarty, C. (1999). *Masks: Faces of culture.* New York: Harry N. Abrams, Inc.

Otto, W.F. (1965). R. Palmer, Trans. *Dionysus, myth and cult.* Bloomington, IN: Indiana University Press.

Pearson, C. (1991). *Awakening the Heroes Within: Twelve Archetypes to Help Us Find Ourselves and Transform Our World.* San Francisco: HarperCollins.

Perera, S.B. (1981). *Descent to the goddess: A way of initiation for women.* Toronto: Inner City Books.

Perera, S.B. (1986). *The scapegoat complex: Toward a mythology of shadow and guilt.* Toronto: Inner City Books.

Phillips, R.P. (1978). Masking in Mende Sande society initiation rituals. *Journal of the International African Institute.* Vol. 48, No. 3 p. 265-277. Edinburgh: Edinburgh University Press. Retrieved from: http://www.jstor.org/stable/1158468.

Pinchbeck, D. (2006). *2012: The return of Quetzacoatle.* New York: Penguin Group USA.

Prattis, I. (n.d.) *Understanding symbolic process – metaphor, vibration, and form.* Ottawa, Canada. Carleton University. Retrieved from: http://www.ianprattis.com/pdf/understandingsymbolic.pdf

Raff, J. (2000). *Jung and the alchemical imagination.* Lakeworth, FL: Nicolas-Hays Inc.

Raff, J. (2003). *The wedding of Sophia: The divine feminine in psychoidal alchemy.* Berwick, ME: Nicolas Hayes, Inc.

Ritzenthaler, R.E. (1969). *Iroquois false-face masks.* Milwaukee, WI: Milwaukee Public Museum

Robertson, R. (1987). *C.G. Jung and the archetypes of the collective unconscious.* New York: P. Lang.

Romanyshyn, R. D. (2009). *The metaphor of alchemy and the alchemy of metaphor: Working in the space between presence and absence.* London: British Association of Psychotherapists. Retrieved from: http://www.robertromanyshyn.com.

Ronnberg, A. & Martin, K. (Eds). (2010) *The book of symbols: Reflections on archetypal images.* The Archive for Research in Archetypal Symbolism. Cologne, Germany: Taschen.

Samuels, A., Shorter, B. & Plaut, A. (1983/2003). *A critical dictionary of Jungian analysis.* London: Routledge

Santrock, J.W. (1982/2007). *Child Development*. New York: McGraw Hill, Inc.

Schechner R.& Schuman, M. (Eds). (1976) *Ritual, play, and performance: readings in the social sciences and theatre*. New York: Seabury Press.

Schierse Leonard, L. (1983). *The wounded woman: Healing the father-daughter relationship*. Boulder, CO: Shambhala Publications, Inc.

Schwartz-Salant, N. (1995). *Jung on alchemy*. Princeton, NJ: Princeton University Press.

Seed, J., Macy, J., Fleming, P. & Naess, A. (1988/2007). *Thinking like a mountain: Towards a council of all beings*. Gabriola Island, BC, Canada: New Catalyst Books.

Shalit, E. (2008). *Enemy, Cripple, and Beggar: Shadows in the hero's path*. Carmel, CA: Fisher King Press.

Shorter, B. (1996). *Susceptible to the sacred: The psychological experience of ritual*. New York: Routledge.

Sidoli, M. (2001). *When the body speaks*. London: Taylor & Francis Ltd.

Simon, E. (2003). *Masking unmasked: Four approaches to basic acting*. New York: Palgrave MacMillan.

Singer, J. (1972). *Boundaries of the soul: The practice of Jung's psychology*. New York: Anchor Press/Doubleday.

Stein, M. (1998, 2009). *Jung's map of the soul*. Peru IL: Open Court Publishing Company.

Stevens, A. (1998). *Ariadne's clue: A guide to the symbols of humankind*. Princeton, NJ: Princeton University Press.

Stevens, A. (1982). *Archetypes, a Natural History of the Self*. New York: Morrow.

Taylor, F.S., (1992). *Alchemists, Founders of Modern Chemistry.* Whitefish, MT: Kessinger Publishing, LLC

Turner, V. & Turner, E. (1978). *Image and Pilgrimage in Christian Culture: Anthropological perspectives.* New York: Columbia University Press.

Turner, V. (1982). *From ritual to theater: The human seriousness of play.* New York: PAJ Publications.

Von Franz, M.L, & Boa, F. (1987). *The way of the dream: Marie Louise von Franz in conversation with Fraser Boa.* Toronto: Windrose Films.

Von Franz, M.L. (1972). *Patterns of creativity mirrored in creation myths.* Dallas, TX: Spring Publications, Inc.

Von Franz, M.L. (1974, 1995) *Shadow and evil in fairy tales.* Boston: Shambhala Publications, Inc.

Von Franz, M.L. (1980). *Psychological Meaning of Redemption Motifs in Fairytales.*

Weinrib, E. (1991). Diagram of the psyche. *Journal of Sandplay Therapy.* Vol. 1. No. 1. Autumn, 1991.

Whitmont, E. (1984). *Return of the Goddess.* New York: Crossroads.

Wilkinson, P. (2009). *Myths and legends: An illustrated guide to their origins and meanings.* New York: DK Publishing.

Wilkinson, R. H. (2003). *The complete gods and goddesses of ancient Egypt.* London: Thames & Hudson.

Winnicott, D.W. (1951/1996). D. Scharff, (Ed.), Transitional Objects and Transitional Phenomena. *Object relations theory and practice: An introduction.* Northvale, NJ: Jason Aronson, Inc.

Wolkenstein, D & Kramer, S.N. (1983). *Inanna queen of heaven and earth: Her stories and hymns from Sumer.* New York: Harper & Row Publishers, Inc.

Woodman, M. (1982). *Addiction to perfection: The still unravished bride.* Toronto: Inner City Books.

ABOUT THE AUTHOR

Tina Azaria, MA is an artist, poet and personal transformation expert specializing in depth psychological and arts-based healing work with individuals and groups. She is the founder of Alembic Arts, an integrative healing and counseling practice, and is the author of *Sprung, Poetry of Emergence*. Tina's work focuses on the use of symbolic and mystery traditions for healing, transformation and growth, and is informed by her work with indigenous healers from around the globe. Learn more at AlembicArts.com

www.ingramcontent.com/pod-product-compliance
Lightning Source LLC
Chambersburg PA
CBHW020529270326
41927CB00006B/508